全国各类成人高等学校招生
考试大纲

专科起点升本科

2024 年版

教育部教育考试院
制订

法学
教育学

中国教育出版传媒集团
高等教育出版社·北京

图书在版编目(C I P)数据

全国各类成人高等学校招生考试大纲.专科起点升本科.法学 教育学:2024 年版 / 教育部教育考试院制订. --北京:高等教育出版社,2024.4

ISBN 978 - 7 - 04 - 061997 - 3

Ⅰ.①全… Ⅱ.①教… Ⅲ.①法学-成人高等教育-入学考试-考试大纲②教育学-成人高等教育-入学考试-考试大纲 Ⅳ.①G724.4

中国国家版本馆 CIP 数据核字(2024)第 055386 号

全国各类成人高等学校招生考试大纲(专科起点升本科)
法学 教育学(2024 年版)
QUANGUO GELEI CHENGREN GAODENG XUEXIAO ZHAOSHENG KAOSHI DAGANG (ZHUANKE QIDIAN SHENG BENKE) FAXUE JIAOYUXUE
(2024 NIAN BAN)

策划编辑 殷力鹰 责任编辑 朱丽娜 封面设计 李小璐 版式设计 童 丹
责任校对 张 然 责任印制 刘思涵

出版发行	高等教育出版社	网　　址	http://www.hep.edu.cn
社　　址	北京市西城区德外大街 4 号		http://www.hep.com.cn
邮政编码	100120	网上订购	http://www.hepmall.com.cn
印　　刷	高教社(天津)印务有限公司		http://www.hepmall.com
开　　本	880 mm×1230 mm 1/32		http://www.hepmall.cn
印　　张	7.625		
字　　数	210 千字	版　　次	2024 年 4 月第 1 版
购书热线	010 - 58581118	印　　次	2024 年 4 月第 1 次印刷
咨询电话	400 - 810 - 0598	定　　价	30.00 元

物 料 号 61997 - 00

说　明

成人高等学历教育是我国高等教育的重要组成部分，担负着为中国式现代化建设培养人才、为广大在职人员继续学习终身学习服务、促进教育强国建设的重要任务。成人高等学校招生全国统一考试（以下简称成人高考）是为各类成人高等学校选拔合格新生而举办的入学考试，自1986年举办以来，共为全国各类成人高等学校选拔了逾6000万名合格新生，为我国成人高等学历教育的发展做出了巨大贡献。《全国各类成人高等学校招生考试大纲》反映党的教育方针、体现成人高等学校新生选拔要求，是指导考试命题和考生复习备考的规范性文件。

为更好地贯彻党的二十大精神，落实立德树人根本任务，培养德智体美劳全面发展的社会主义建设者和接班人，反映成人高考学科内容的发展变化，满足成人高等学校招收培养适应经济社会发展所需人才的需要，教育部有关部门在研究、分析近年全国考生考试情况，充分征求各地招生考试机构和成人高等学校意见的基础上，结合生源群体的变化，对2020年版《全国各类成人高等学校招生考试大纲》（以下简称《大纲》）进行了修订。

修订后的《大纲》为2024年版，包括高中起点升本、专科和专科起点升本科两部分。高中起点升本、专科大纲包括语文、汉语（用于少数民族聚居地区使用民族语文授课的少数民族考生报考用汉语授课的成人高等学校的语文科目考试）、数学、英语、日语、俄语、物理化学、历史地理8个科目，共1册；专科起点升本科大纲包括英语、政治、大学语文、艺术概论、高等数学（一）、高等数学（二）、民法、教育理论、生态学基础和医学综合10个科目，为方便报考不同学科专业的考生复习，分为5册。

本册书为《专科起点升本科 法学 教育学 考试大纲》，供报考法学和教育学（职业教育类除外）各专业的考生使用。

2024 年 3 月

目　　录

政治 …… 1

　总要求 …… 1

　考试内容 …… 1

　考试形式及试卷结构 …… 22

　样题 …… 23

英语 …… 31

　总要求 …… 31

　考试内容 …… 31

　考试形式及试卷结构 …… 33

　样题 …… 34

　附录　词汇表 …… 49

民法 …… 117

　总要求 …… 117

　考试内容 …… 117

　考试形式及试卷结构 …… 155

　样题 …… 155

教育理论 …… 163

　总要求 …… 163

　考试内容 …… 164

　考试形式及试卷结构 …… 228

　样题 …… 229

政　治

总　要　求

政治学科考试反映对考生的思想政治理论水平的基本要求。考生在理论学习和实践锻炼的基础上，应当确立正确政治方向，树立中国特色社会主义理想信念，培育社会主义核心价值观，掌握马克思主义的世界观和方法论，成为德智体美劳全面发展的社会主义建设者和接班人，立志肩负起全面实现中华民族伟大复兴中国梦的时代重任。考生应能：

1. 识记并理解马克思主义哲学、毛泽东思想和中国特色社会主义理论体系、习近平新时代中国特色社会主义思想的基本概念、基本观点和基本原理及其重要意义。

2. 运用马克思主义哲学、毛泽东思想和中国特色社会主义理论体系、习近平新时代中国特色社会主义思想的基本原理和基本方法，分析、论证、阐释建设中国特色社会主义实践的重要问题。

3. 使用学科术语，清晰明了、合乎逻辑地表达观点、阐述问题。

考试内容

第一部分　马克思主义哲学原理

一、马克思主义哲学是科学的世界观和方法论

【要求】

了解哲学、世界观、马克思主义哲学等基本概念。理解唯物主义与

唯心主义、辩证法与形而上学的对立、马克思主义哲学产生的社会历史条件、马克思主义哲学的基本特征。掌握哲学基本问题及其内容，学习马克思主义哲学的方法，自觉以马克思主义哲学作为行动指南。

（一）哲学及其基本问题

1. 哲学与世界观、方法论

2. 哲学的基本问题

3. 哲学的主要派别

（二）马克思主义哲学及其基本特征

1. 马克思主义哲学的创立与发展

2. 马克思主义哲学的基本特征

3. 马克思主义哲学是认识世界和改造世界的伟大工具

二、世界的多样性与物质统一性

【要求】

了解物质、运动、静止、时间、空间、意识、规律、一元论、二元论等基本概念。理解辩证唯物主义的物质范畴及其理论意义，理解物质与运动、物质运动与时间和空间、运动与静止、客观世界与主观世界、意识与人工智能的关系。掌握物质与意识、主观能动性与客观规律性的辩证关系、世界的物质统一性原理及其意义。

（一）物质及其存在方式

1. 哲学的物质范畴

2. 物质的存在方式

3. 物质世界的二重化

（二）物质与意识的辩证关系

1. 物质决定意识

2. 意识对物质具有反作用

3. 主观能动性与客观规律性的辩证统一

4. 意识与人工智能

（三）世界的物质统一性

1. 世界的物质统一性的表现

2. 世界的物质统一性原理的理论意义和实践意义

三、事物的普遍联系和变化发展

【要求】

了解联系、发展、新事物、矛盾、矛盾的同一性、矛盾的斗争性、矛盾的普遍性、矛盾的特殊性、度、量变、质变、否定之否定等基本概念。理解联系的特点、发展的实质、唯物辩证法的总观点和总特征、唯物辩证法的实质和核心、唯物辩证法是认识世界和改造世界的根本方法。掌握唯物辩证法基本规律的主要内容、唯物辩证法的基本范畴及各对范畴的辩证关系，能运用唯物辩证法分析、解决实际问题，增强思维能力。

（一）联系和发展的普遍性

1. 事物的普遍联系

2. 事物的变化发展

（二）唯物辩证法的基本规律

1. 对立统一规律是事物发展的根本规律

2. 量变质变规律

3. 否定之否定规律

（三）联系和发展的基本环节

1. 内容与形式

2. 本质与现象

3. 原因与结果

4. 必然与偶然

5. 现实与可能

（四）唯物辩证法是认识世界和改造世界的根本方法

1. 唯物辩证法的本质特征和认识功能

2. 学习唯物辩证法，不断增强思维能力

四、实践与认识及其发展规律

【要求】

了解实践、认识、主体、客体、真理、谬误、价值等基本概念。理解科学的实践观及其意义，实践的基本特征、基本结构和基本形式，实践对认识的决定作用，主体与客体的关系，辩证唯物主义认识论与唯心主义认识论的对立以及与旧唯物主义认识论的区别，实践与认识的辩证运动及其规律，真理的两种属性，价值的基本特征，真理与价值的辩证统一，认识世界和改造世界的辩证关系，马克思主义认识论与党的思想路线的关系。掌握感性认识与理性认识辩证关系的原理、真理的绝对性和相对性辩证统一的原理、实践是检验真理的唯一标准的原理及其意义，树立正确的价值观。

（一）实践与认识

1. 科学的实践观及其意义

2. 实践的本质与基本结构

3. 认识的本质与过程

4. 实践与认识的辩证运动及其规律

（二）真理与价值

1. 真理的客观性、绝对性和相对性

2. 真理的检验标准

3. 真理与价值的辩证统一

（三）认识世界和改造世界

1. 认识世界和改造世界及其辩证关系

2. 一切从实际出发，实事求是

3. 坚持守正创新，实现理论创新和实践创新的良性互动

五、历史观的基本问题和人类社会的存在与发展

【要求】

了解社会存在、生产方式、社会意识、意识形态、生产力、生产关系、经济基础、上层建筑、国家、交往、社会形态、文明等基本概念。理解唯心史观的主要缺陷、唯物史观创立的伟大意义、自然地理环境对人类社会生存和发展的作用、人口因素对社会发展的影响和制约、生产方式是社会历史发展的决定力量、社会意识的复杂结构。掌握社会存在和社会意识的辩证关系原理及其意义、生产力与生产关系的矛盾运动及其

规律、经济基础与上层建筑的矛盾运动及其规律，能用唯物史观认识人类社会历史及其发展。

（一）两种根本对立的历史观

1. 历史观的基本问题

2. 唯心史观的主要缺陷

3. 唯物史观创立的伟大意义

（二）社会存在与社会意识

1. 社会存在及其在社会发展中的作用

2. 社会意识及其结构

3. 社会存在和社会意识的辩证关系原理及其意义

（三）生产力与生产关系的矛盾运动及其规律

1. 生产力与生产关系

2. 生产关系一定要适合生产力状况的规律

（四）经济基础与上层建筑的矛盾运动及其规律

1. 经济基础与上层建筑

2. 上层建筑一定要适合经济基础状况的规律

（五）人类普遍交往与世界历史的形成发展

1. 交往及其作用

2. 世界历史的形成和发展

（六）社会进步与社会形态更替

1. 社会进步与人的发展

2. 社会形态的内涵

3. 社会形态更替的统一性与多样性

4. 社会形态更替的必然性与选择性

（七）文明及其多样性

1. 文明及其演进

2. 文明的多样性

六、社会历史发展的动力

【要求】

了解社会基本矛盾、阶级、社会革命、人民群众、历史人物等基本概念。理解社会基本矛盾、阶级斗争、社会革命、改革、科学技术以及文化在社会发展中的作用。掌握社会主要矛盾及其转化的原理、马克思主义的阶级分析方法、人民群众是历史创造者的原理、无产阶级政党的群众路线、评价历史人物的正确方法。

（一）社会基本矛盾在历史发展中的作用

1. 生产力和生产关系的矛盾、经济基础和上层建筑的矛盾是社会基本矛盾

2. 社会基本矛盾是社会发展的根本动力

3. 社会基本矛盾与社会主要矛盾

（二）阶级斗争和社会革命在社会发展中的作用

1. 阶级斗争是阶级社会发展的直接动力

2. 阶级社会中革命对社会发展的作用

3. 马克思主义的阶级分析方法是认识阶级社会的科学方法

4. 改革在社会发展中的作用

（三）科学技术在社会发展中的作用

1. 科技革命是推动经济和社会发展的强大杠杆

2. 正确把握科学技术的社会作用

（四）文化在社会发展中的作用

1. 文化对社会发展起着促进或阻碍、加快或延缓的作用

2. 把握文化的正确方向，发挥文化的积极作用

（五）人民群众在历史发展中的作用

1. 英雄史观与群众史观的对立

2. 人民群众在创造历史过程中的决定作用

3. 无产阶级政党的群众路线

4. 历史人物的历史作用及评价

5. 群众、阶级、政党、领袖的关系

第二部分　毛泽东思想和中国特色社会主义理论体系概论

一、马克思主义中国化时代化的历史进程与理论成果

【要求】

了解马克思主义中国化时代化的提出和内涵。理解马克思主义中国化时代化的历史进程。掌握马克思主义中国化时代化理论成果及其关系。

（一）马克思主义中国化时代化的提出

（二）马克思主义中国化时代化的内涵

（三）马克思主义中国化时代化的历史进程

（四）马克思主义中国化时代化理论成果及其关系

二、毛泽东思想及其历史地位

【要求】

了解毛泽东思想产生和发展的社会历史条件和历史过程。理解毛泽东思想的历史地位与指导意义。掌握毛泽东思想的科学内涵、主要内容及活的灵魂。

（一）毛泽东思想的形成和发展

1. 毛泽东思想形成发展的历史条件

2. 毛泽东思想形成发展的过程

（二）毛泽东思想的主要内容和活的灵魂

1. 毛泽东思想的主要内容

2. 毛泽东思想活的灵魂

（三）毛泽东思想的历史地位

三、新民主主义革命理论

【要求】

了解新民主主义革命理论的形成，掌握新民主主义革命的总路线、基本纲领和革命道路的基本内容、新民主主义革命的基本经验和新民

主主义革命理论的意义。

（一）新民主主义革命理论形成的依据

1. 近代中国国情和中国革命的时代特征

2. 新民主主义革命理论的实践基础

（二）新民主主义革命的总路线和基本纲领

1. 新民主主义革命的总路线

2. 新民主主义的基本纲领

（三）新民主主义革命的道路和基本经验

1. 新民主主义革命的道路

2. 新民主主义革命的三大法宝

3. 新民主主义革命理论的意义

四、社会主义改造理论

【要求】

了解从新民主主义转变到社会主义的历史必然性，理解社会主义改造道路和历史经验，掌握社会主义基本制度在中国的确立及其重大意义。

（一）从新民主主义到社会主义的转变

1. 新民主主义社会是一个过渡性的社会

2. 党在过渡时期的总路线及其依据

（二）社会主义改造道路和历史经验

1. 适合中国特点的社会主义改造道路

2. 社会主义改造的历史经验

（三）社会主义基本制度在中国的确立

1. 社会主义基本制度的确立及其理论根据

2. 确立社会主义基本制度的重大意义

五、社会主义建设道路初步探索的理论成果

【要求】

了解社会主义建设道路初步探索中社会主义经济、政治和文化建设的方针和政策，理解社会主义建设道路初步探索的意义和经验教训，

掌握以毛泽东同志为主要代表的中国共产党人对社会主义建设道路的初步探索及其重要理论成果。

（一）初步探索的重要理论成果

1. 调动一切积极因素为社会主义事业服务

2. 正确认识和处理社会主义社会矛盾的思想

3. 走中国工业化道路的思想

4. 初步探索的其他理论成果

（二）初步探索的意义和经验教训

1. 初步探索的意义

2. 初步探索的经验教训

六、中国特色社会主义理论体系的形成发展

【要求】

了解中国特色社会主义理论体系形成发展的社会历史条件，理解中国特色社会主义理论体系形成发展过程。

（一）中国特色社会主义理论体系形成发展的社会历史条件

1. 中国特色社会主义理论体系形成发展的国际背景

2. 中国特色社会主义理论体系形成发展的历史条件

（二）中国特色社会主义理论体系形成发展过程

1. 中国特色社会主义理论体系的形成

2. 中国特色社会主义理论体系的跨世纪发展

3. 中国特色社会主义理论体系在新世纪新阶段的新发展

4. 中国特色社会主义理论体系在新时代的新篇章

七、邓小平理论

【要求】

理解邓小平理论首要的基本的理论问题、精髓和主要内容，掌握邓小平理论的历史地位。

（一）邓小平理论首要的基本的理论问题和精髓

1. 邓小平理论首要的基本的理论问题

2. 邓小平理论的精髓

（二）邓小平理论的主要内容

1. 社会主义初级阶段理论和党的基本路线

2. 社会主义根本任务和发展战略理论

3. 社会主义改革开放和社会主义市场经济理论

4. “两手抓，两手都要硬”

5. “一国两制”与祖国统一

6. 中国特色社会主义外交和国际战略

7. 党的建设理论

（三）邓小平理论的历史地位

八、“三个代表”重要思想

【要求】

掌握“三个代表”重要思想的核心观点、主要内容和历史地位。

（一）“三个代表”重要思想的核心观点

1. 始终代表中国先进生产力的发展要求

2. 始终代表中国先进文化的发展方向

3. 始终代表中国最广大人民的根本利益

（二）“三个代表”重要思想的主要内容

1. 发展是党执政兴国的第一要务

2. 建立社会主义市场经济体制

3. 全面建设小康社会

4. 建设社会主义政治文明

5. 实施“引进来”和“走出去”相结合的对外开放战略

6. 推进党的建设新的伟大工程

（三）“三个代表”重要思想的历史地位

九、科学发展观

【要求】

掌握科学发展观的科学内涵、主要内容和历史地位。

（一）科学发展观的科学内涵

1. 推动经济社会发展是科学发展观的第一要义

2. 以人为本是科学发展观的核心立场

3. 全面协调可持续是科学发展观的基本要求

4. 统筹兼顾是科学发展观的根本方法

（二）科学发展观的主要内容

1. 加快转变经济发展方式

2. 发展社会主义民主政治

3. 推进社会主义文化强国建设

4. 构建社会主义和谐社会

5. 推进生态文明建设

6. 全面提高党的建设科学化水平

（三）科学发展观的历史地位

第三部分　习近平新时代中国特色社会主义思想概论

一、习近平新时代中国特色社会主义思想的创立

【要求】

了解习近平新时代中国特色社会主义思想创立的时代背景，理解“两个结合”的基本含义，掌握习近平新时代中国特色社会主义思想的科学体系，把握习近平新时代中国特色社会主义思想的历史地位和“两个确立”的决定性意义。

（一）习近平新时代中国特色社会主义思想创立的时代背景

（二）习近平新时代中国特色社会主义思想是“两个结合”的重大成果

（三）习近平新时代中国特色社会主义思想是完整的科学体系

（四）习近平新时代中国特色社会主义思想的历史地位和“两个确立”的决定性意义

二、新时代坚持和发展中国特色社会主义

【要求】

了解中国特色社会主义开创和发展的历程，理解中国特色社会主义的深刻内涵和重要意义，掌握中国特色社会主义进入新时代的科学内涵和意义，理解“五位一体”总体布局和“四个全面”战略布局，把握党的基本理论、基本路线、基本方略，坚定“四个自信”。

（一）中国特色社会主义的深刻内涵和重要意义

（二）坚定道路自信、理论自信、制度自信、文化自信

（三）中国特色社会主义进入新时代

1. 中国特色社会主义新时代是我国发展新的历史方位

2. 社会主要矛盾变化是关系全局的历史性变化

3. 新时代伟大变革及其里程碑意义

（四）中国特色社会主义事业总体布局和战略布局

（五）党的基本理论、基本路线、基本方略

三、以中国式现代化全面推进中华民族伟大复兴

【要求】

了解中华民族伟大复兴中国梦的提出、科学内涵和实现途径，理解全面建成小康社会的里程碑意义，理解全面建成社会主义现代化强国的战略安排，掌握中国式现代化的中国特色、本质要求，掌握推进中国式现代化需要牢牢把握的重大原则和需要正确处理的重大关系，把握中国式现代化创造了人类文明新形态。

（一）中华民族近代以来最伟大的梦想

1. 实现中华民族伟大复兴的中国梦

2. 在中华大地上全面建成小康社会

3. 全面建成社会主义现代化强国

（二）中国式现代化是强国建设、民族复兴的唯一正确道路

1. 中国式现代化是中国共产党领导人民长期探索和实践的重大成果

2. 中国式现代化的中国特色和本质要求

3. 中国式现代化创造了人类文明新形态

4. 推进中国式现代化需要牢牢把握的重大原则和需要正确处理的重大关系

5. 推进中国式现代化必须坚持团结奋斗

四、坚持党的全面领导

【要求】

了解中国最大的国情就是中国共产党的领导，理解中国共产党的领导是全面的、系统的、整体的，理解党的领导制度是我国的根本领导制度，掌握中国共产党领导是中国特色社会主义最本质的特征、中国共产党领导是中国特色社会主义制度的最大优势、中国共产党是最高政治领导力量。

（一）中国共产党领导是中国特色社会主义最本质的特征

1. 中国最大的国情就是中国共产党的领导

2. 中国共产党领导是中国特色社会主义制度的最大优势

3. 加强党的全面领导为新时代党和国家事业发展提供了坚强保证

（二）坚持党对一切工作的领导

1. 中国共产党是最高政治领导力量

2. 党的领导是全面的、系统的、整体的

3. 维护党中央权威和集中统一领导

（三）健全和完善党的领导制度体系

1. 党的领导制度是我国的根本领导制度

2. 健全党中央对重大工作的领导体制

3. 健全党的全面领导制度

五、坚持以人民为中心

【要求】

了解人民是历史的创造者，是真正的英雄，理解“江山就是人民，人民就是江山”的深刻内涵，掌握坚持人民至上的内涵和意义，把握全面落实以人民为中心的发展思想。

（一）江山就是人民，人民就是江山

1. 人民是历史的创造者，是真正的英雄

2. 人民立场是中国共产党的根本政治立场

（二）坚持人民至上

1. 人民对美好生活的向往就是党的奋斗目标

2. 依靠人民创造历史伟业

3. 人民是党的工作的最高裁决者和最终评判者

（三）全面落实以人民为中心的发展思想

1. 坚持和贯彻党的群众路线

2. 扎实推进全体人民共同富裕

六、全面深化改革开放

【要求】

了解改革开放的历史进程和重大成就，理解改革开放是决定当代中国命运的关键一招，掌握全面深化改革开放的目标、正确方法论和意义。

（一）改革开放是决定当代中国命运的关键一招

1. 改革开放是我们前进的重要法宝

2. 新时代全面深化改革开放是一场深刻革命

3. 全面深化改革开放的正确方向

（二）统筹推进各领域各方面改革开放

1. 全面深化改革总目标

2. 全面深化改革开放的正确方法论

3. 将改革开放进行到底

七、推动高质量发展

【要求】

了解新时代我国经济发展的形势和任务，理解社会主义基本经济制度，掌握习近平经济思想，把握立足新发展阶段、贯彻新发展理念、构建新发展格局、建设现代化经济体系、推动高质量发展的内涵、意义和举措。

（一）新发展理念

1. 进入新发展阶段

2. 贯彻新发展理念

3. 以新发展理念引领高质量发展

（二）社会主义基本经济制度

1. 坚持公有制为主体、多种所有制经济共同发展

2. 坚持按劳分配为主体、多种分配方式并存

3. 构建高水平社会主义市场经济体制

（三）新发展格局

1. 新发展格局的内涵和意义

2. 深化供给侧结构性改革

3. 推进高水平科技自立自强

（四）现代化经济体系

1. 现代化经济体系的内涵

2. 实施国家重大发展战略

八、社会主义现代化建设的教育、科技、人才战略

【要求】

了解新时代我国教育、科技、人才建设方面的工作和成就，理解科教兴国战略、人才强国战略、创新驱动发展战略的内涵，掌握建设教育强国、科技强国、人才强国的主要内容和重要意义。

（一）全面建设社会主义现代化国家的基础性、战略性支撑

1. 实施科教兴国战略、人才强国战略、创新驱动发展战略

2. 坚持教育优先发展、科技自立自强、人才引领驱动

（二）建设教育强国

（三）建设科技强国

（四）建设人才强国

九、发展全过程人民民主

【要求】

了解全过程人民民主概念的形成，理解巩固和发展新时代爱国统一战线的内涵和意义，掌握中国特色社会主义政治制度的主要内容、全过程人民民主的内涵和重要意义。

（一）坚定中国特色社会主义政治制度自信

1. 人民民主的内涵和重要意义

2. 中国特色社会主义政治制度

3. 中国特色社会主义政治发展道路

（二）全过程人民民主是社会主义民主政治的本质属性

1. 全过程人民民主是社会主义民主政治的伟大创造

2. 全过程人民民主是全链条、全方位、全覆盖的民主

3. 全过程人民民主是最广泛、最真实、最管用的民主

（三）健全人民当家作主的制度体系

1. 人民当家作主的制度体系的内涵

2. 全面发展协商民主

3. 积极发展基层民主

（四）巩固和发展新时代爱国统一战线

1. 统一战线是凝聚人心、汇聚力量的强大法宝

2. 铸牢中华民族共同体意识

3. 加强和促进海内外中华儿女大团结

十、全面依法治国

【要求】

了解全面依法治国的总目标和重大意义，理解中国特色社会主义法治道路的核心要义和基本原则，理解中国特色社会主义法治体系的主要内容，掌握习近平法治思想。

（一）坚持中国特色社会主义法治道路

1. 中国特色社会法治道路的核心要义和基本原则

2. 统筹处理全面依法治国的重大关系
（二）建设中国特色社会主义法治体系
1. 全面推进依法治国的总抓手
2. 坚持依宪治国、依宪执政
3. 推进中国特色社会主义法治体系建设
（三）加快建设法治中国
1. 法治中国建设的总体目标
2. 法治中国建设的工作布局
3. 建设更高水平的法治中国

十一、建设社会主义文化强国

【要求】

了解中华文明的突出特性，理解文化繁荣兴盛和中国特色社会主义文化发展道路的重要性，掌握建设社会主义意识形态和推动社会主义文化建设的主要工作。

（一）文化是民族生存和发展的重要力量
1. 中国特色社会主义文化自信
2. 中国特色社会主义文化发展道路
（二）建设具有强大凝聚力和引领力的社会主义意识形态
1. 坚持马克思主义在意识形态领域指导地位的根本制度
2. 加强马克思主义理论建设
3. 塑造主流舆论新格局
（三）推动社会主义文化建设
1. 践行社会主义核心价值观
2. 弘扬中国共产党人精神谱系
3. 传承发展中华优秀传统文化
4. 提升国家文化软实力和中华文化影响力

十二、以保障和改善民生为重点加强社会建设

【要求】

了解社会建设的工作和成就，理解提高人民生活品质的主要着力点，掌握在发展中增进民生福祉的意义和举措，把握推进社会治理现代化的主要内容和重要意义。

（一）促进人民生活幸福

1. 民生是人民幸福之基

2. 增强人民获得感幸福感安全感

3. 坚持在发展中增进民生福祉

（二）提高人民生活品质

1. 完善分配制度

2. 实施就业优先战略

3. 健全社会保障体系

4. 推进健康中国建设

（三）推进社会治理现代化

1. 加强和创新社会治理

2. 完善社会治理体系

十三、建设社会主义生态文明

【要求】

了解生态文明建设的巨大成就，理解绿水青山就是金山银山的科学内涵，掌握生态文明建设的重要意义、建设美丽中国的主要任务和全球环境治理的中国方案，掌握习近平生态文明思想。

（一）坚持人与自然和谐共生

1. 生态文明建设的重要意义和巨大成就

2. 绿水青山就是金山银山

（二）建设美丽中国

1. 加快形成绿色生产方式和生活方式

2. 坚持山水林田湖草沙一体化保护和系统治理

3. 用最严格制度最严密法治保护生态环境

（三）共谋全球生态文明建设之路

1. 保护人类共同家园

2. 共建清洁美丽世界

3. 推动全球可持续发展

十四、维护和塑造国家安全

【要求】

了解新时代维护和塑造国家安全取得的重要成就，理解构建统筹各领域安全的新安全格局，掌握总体国家安全观的主要内容和重要意义。

（一）坚持总体国家安全观

1. 国家安全是民族复兴的根基

2. 总体国家安全观是新时代国家安全工作的基本遵循

（二）构建统筹各领域安全的新安全格局

1. 统筹发展和安全

2. 把维护政治安全放在首要位置

3. 维护重点领域国家安全

（三）开创新时代国家安全工作新局面

1. 推进国家安全体系和能力现代化

2. 建设更高水平的平安中国

3. 提高防范化解重大风险能力

十五、建设巩固国防和强大人民军队

【要求】

了解国防和军队建设的重要意义，理解党在新时代的强军目标和科学内涵，理解全面推进国防和军队现代化的战略安排和举措，掌握习近平强军思想。

（一）强国必须强军，军强才能国安

1. 国防和军队建设的重要意义

2. 新时代人民军队使命任务

（二）实现党在新时代的强军目标

1. 强军目标的科学内涵

2. 全面推进国防和军队现代化的战略安排

（三）加快推进国防和军队现代化

1. 坚持党对人民军队的绝对领导

2. 开创国防和军队现代化新局面的举措

3. 加强练兵备战

4. 提高一体化国家战略体系和能力

十六、坚持“一国两制”和推进祖国完全统一

【要求】

了解“一国两制”的形成和发展，理解“一国两制”的科学内涵和重大意义，理解新时代“一国两制”在香港、澳门的成功实践，掌握新时代党解决台湾问题的总体方略。

（一）全面准确理解和贯彻“一国两制”方针

1. “一国两制”是中国特色社会主义的伟大创举

2. 准确把握“一国两制”的科学内涵

3. 坚持和完善“一国两制”制度体系

（二）保持香港、澳门长期繁荣稳定

1. 香港、澳门保持长期稳定发展良好态势

2. 推动香港进入由乱到治走向由治及兴的新阶段

3. 支持香港、澳门融入国家发展大局

（三）推进祖国完全统一

1. 实现祖国完全统一是中华民族伟大复兴的必然要求

2. 坚持贯彻新时代党解决台湾问题的总体方略

3. 牢牢把握两岸关系主导权和主动权

十七、中国特色大国外交和推动构建人类命运共同体

【要求】

了解新时代中国外交的巨大成就，理解中国特色大国外交的内涵

和举措，掌握构建人类命运共同体的内涵、意义和举措，掌握习近平外交思想。

（一）新时代中国外交在大变局中开创新局

1. 当今世界正经历百年未有之大变局

2. 中国必须有自己特色的大国外交

（二）全面推进中国特色大国外交

1. 坚持走和平发展道路

2. 推动构建新型国际关系

3. 坚决维护国家主权、安全、发展利益

4. 坚持外交为民

（三）推动构建人类命运共同体

1. 构建人类命运共同体的内涵和意义

2. 推动构建人类命运共同体的价值基础和重要依托

3. 积极参与全球治理体系改革和建设

4. 高质量共建"一带一路"

十八、全面从严治党

【要求】

了解新时代全面从严治党的巨大成就，理解新时代党的建设总要求，掌握新时代党的建设新的伟大工程，掌握习近平关于党的建设的重要思想。

（一）全面从严治党是新时代党的建设的鲜明主题

1. 加强党的自身建设的必要性

2. 坚定不移全面从严治党

（二）以政治建设为统领深入推进党的建设

1. 把党的政治建设摆在首位

2. 思想建设是党的基础性建设

3. 贯彻新时代党的组织路线

4. 以严的基调强化正风肃纪

5. 把制度建设贯穿到党的各项建设之中

（三）坚定不移推进反腐败斗争

1. 腐败是党长期执政面临的最大威胁

2. 坚持标本兼治开展反腐败斗争

3. 反腐败必须永远吹冲锋号

（四）建设长期执政的马克思主义政党

1. 党的自我革命是跳出历史周期率的第二个答案

2. 时刻保持解决大党独有难题的清醒和坚定

3. 以伟大自我革命引领伟大社会革命

第四部分 时事政治

【要求】

了解年度间（上一年 7 月 1 日至考试当年 6 月 30 日）国际国内重大时事。

了解中国共产党和中国政府在现阶段的基本路线和重大方针政策。

考试形式及试卷结构

试卷总分：150 分

考试时间：150 分钟

考试方式：闭卷、笔试

试卷内容比例：

马克思主义哲学原理	约 27％
毛泽东思想和中国特色社会主义理论体系概论	约 33％
习近平新时代中国特色社会主义思想概论	约 33％
时事政治	约 7％

试卷题型结构：

选择题	35 小题，每小题 2 分，共 70 分
简答题	4 小题，每小题 10 分，共 40 分

论述题　　　　　　　　　2 小题,每小题 20 分,共 40 分

样　　题

一、**选择题**:1～35 小题,每小题 2 分,共 70 分。在每小题给出的四个选项中,选出一项最符合题目要求的。

1. 思维和存在的关系问题是

A. 全部哲学的基本问题　　B. 历史观的基本问题

C. 思想路线的核心问题　　D. 辩证法的核心问题

2. 马克思主义的产生具有深刻的思想渊源。作为马克思主义哲学直接理论来源的是

A. 古希腊罗马哲学　　B. 近代英国哲学

C. 近代法国哲学　　D. 德国古典哲学

3. “笑一笑十年少,愁一愁白了头”表明意识具有

A. 目的性

B. 指导实践改造客观世界的作用

C. 创造性

D. 调控人的行为和生理活动的作用

4. 人类社会是物质存在的一种特定形态,人的意识统一于物质,这是

A. 主观唯心主义的观点　　B. 辩证唯物主义的观点

C. 客观唯心主义的观点　　D. 庸俗唯物主义的观点

5. 对立统一规律提供的认识世界和改造世界的根本方法是

A. 阶级分析方法　　B. 历史分析方法

C. 矛盾分析方法　　D. 逻辑分析方法

6. 下列选项中体现事物因果联系的是

A. 有无相生　　B. 过犹不及

C. 冬去春来　　D. 摩擦生热

7. 否定之否定规律揭示了事物的发展是

A. 绝对性与相对性的统一　　B. 有限性与无限性的统一

C. 前进性与曲折性的统一　　D. 稳定性与变动性的统一

8. 观念上层建筑指的是

A. 意识形态　　B. 政治制度

C. 法律制度　　D. 政治组织

9. 马克思主义认为，社会革命根源于

A. 人口数量和结构的变化

B. 思想观念斗争的尖锐化

C. 自然资源和环境的变化

D. 社会基本矛盾的尖锐化

10. 实践是人类能动地改造世界的社会性的物质活动，其基本特征是客观实在性、自觉能动性以及

A. 社会历史性　　B. 主观创造性

C. 主体多元性　　D. 目标单一性

11. 毛泽东思想开始萌芽的标志是

A. 人民民主专政理论的形成

B. 关于新民主主义革命基本思想的提出

C. 农村包围城市、武装夺取政权道路的开辟

D. 马克思主义中国化第一次历史性飞跃的实现

12. 新民主主义革命的主力军是

A. 无产阶级　　B. 小资产阶级

C. 农民　　D. 知识分子

13. 过渡时期总路线中，“过渡时期”是指

A. 从资本主义社会向社会主义社会过渡

B. 从封建社会向半殖民地半封建社会演变

C. 从半殖民地半封建社会向资本主义社会转变

D. 从中华人民共和国成立到社会主义改造基本完成

14. 在社会主义社会两类社会矛盾中，工人阶级同民族资产阶级的矛盾是

A. 敌我矛盾　　B. 人民内部矛盾

C. 基本矛盾　　D. 社会主要矛盾

15. 毛泽东中国工业化道路思想强调，实现四个现代化关键在于

A. 农业现代化 B. 工业现代化
C. 国防现代化 D. 科学技术现代化

16. 改革开放以来，我们党和国家生存发展的政治基石是
A. 四项基本原则 B. 以德治国
C. 国际政治秩序 D. 依宪治国

17. 邓小平指出，中国解决所有问题的关键是
A. 要靠照搬马克思主义理论 B. 要靠自己的发展
C. 要靠模仿周边国家的经验 D. 要靠别国的支持

18. “三个代表”重要思想强调，我们党进行的一切奋斗，归根到底都是为了
A. 社会生产力的快速发展
B. 社会主义和谐社会的建成
C. 最广大人民的根本利益
D. 社会主义市场经济的完善

19. 坚持中国特色社会主义政治发展道路，最根本的是
A. 坚持改革、发展、稳定的辩证统一
B. 坚持生产发展、生活富裕、生态良好的有机统一
C. 坚持党的使命、国家的前途、人民的福祉的辩证统一
D. 坚持党的领导、人民当家作主、依法治国的有机统一

20. 社会主义核心价值观中，富强、民主、文明、和谐体现的是
A. 国家层面的价值要求 B. 社会层面的价值要求
C. 公民层面的价值要求 D. 组织层面的价值要求

21. 党的十八大以来，我们党的全部理论和实践探索都是
A. 围绕推动高质量发展来展开、深化和拓展的
B. 围绕全面建成小康社会来展开、深化和拓展的
C. 围绕坚持和发展中国特色社会主义来展开、深化和拓展的
D. 围绕传承和弘扬中华优秀传统文化来展开、深化和拓展的

22. 中国特色社会主义事业总体布局和战略布局分别是
A. “两个转变”和“一体两翼”
B. “五位一体”和“四个全面”

C. “八个明确”和“四面八方”

D. “一个中心”和“五湖四海”

23. 习近平新时代中国特色社会主义思想的根本立场是

A. 人民立场　　B. 阶级立场

C. 历史自觉　　D. 求真务实

24. 习近平指出:“实现中国梦必须走中国道路、弘扬中国精神、凝聚中国力量。”中国力量指的是

A. 科技创新的力量　　B. 文化创新的力量

C. 全国各族人民大团结的力量　　D. 全世界人民大团结的力量

25. 全面建设社会主义现代化国家的进程分两个阶段来安排,其中第二个阶段的目标是到本世纪中叶

A. 实现总体小康

B. 消除绝对贫困

C. 人均国内生产总值达到中等发达国家的水平

D. 把我国建成富强民主文明和谐美丽的社会主义现代化强国

26. 在新发展理念中,注重解决发展不平衡问题的是

A. 创新发展　　B. 协调发展

C. 绿色发展　　D. 共享发展

27. 构建新发展格局明确了我国经济现代化的路径选择。新发展格局指的是

A. 坚持“两个毫不动摇”

B. 市场和资源“两头在外”的发展格局

C. 以国内大循环为主体、国内国际双循环相互促进

D. 发挥市场在资源配置中的决定性作用和更好发挥政府作用

28. 新时代推进全面依法治国的总抓手是

A. 坚持以人民为中心

B. 建设中国特色社会主义法治体系

C. 坚持统筹推进国内法治和涉外法治

D. 坚持依法治国、依法执政、依法行政共同推进

29. 总体国家安全观明确,国家安全的宗旨和根本分别是

A. 人民安全和政治安全　　　　B. 科技安全和网络安全
C. 经济安全和生态安全　　　　D. 资源安全和太空安全

30. 习近平强军思想中，反映军队的根本职能和军队建设的根本指向的是

A. 能打胜仗　　　　B. 作风优良
C. 听党指挥　　　　D. 军民融合

31. 2022 年 8 月 28 日开工建设的西部陆海新通道骨干工程——平陆运河位于

A. 四川　　　　B. 云南
C. 贵州　　　　D. 广西

32. 党的二十大要求，全党同志务必不忘初心、牢记使命，务必谦虚谨慎、艰苦奋斗，务必

A. 敢于斗争、善于斗争　　　　B. 增强自信、继续前进
C. 自信自强、守正创新　　　　D. 踔厉奋发、勇毅前行

33. 2023 年 3 月 26 日，与我国建立外交关系的国家是

A. 哥伦比亚　　　　B. 洪都拉斯
C. 南非　　　　D. 古巴

34. 2023 年 5 月 19 日，首届中国—中亚峰会发表《中国—中亚峰会西安宣言》，与会六国决心携手构建

A. 中国—中亚丝路开发银行　　　　B. 中国—中亚自由贸易区
C. 中国—中亚经济合作组织　　　　D. 中国—中亚命运共同体

35. 2023 年 6 月 26 日至 28 日，十四届全国人大常委会第三次会议在北京召开。会议决定将每年 8 月 15 日设立为

A. 全国土地日　　　　B. 国家宪法日
C. 全国生态日　　　　D. 全民健身日

二、简答题：36～39 小题，每小题 10 分，共 40 分。

36. 简述近代中国社会的主要矛盾和历史任务。

37. 邓小平社会主义市场经济理论要点有哪些？

38. 简述科学发展观的科学内涵。

39. 为什么说党的领导是中国特色社会主义最本质的特征？

三、**论述题**：40～41 小题，每小题 20 分，共 40 分。

40. 试述感性认识和理性认识的辩证关系，并说明割裂二者的统一在实际工作中会导致的错误。

41. 党的十八大以来，以习近平同志为核心的党中央牢牢把握中国和世界发展大势，深刻思考人类前途命运，积极推进重大外交理论和实践创新，形成了习近平外交思想，指引外交工作取得全方位、开创性历史成就。试述新时代中国独立自主的和平外交政策的主要内涵。

参考答案

一、选择题

1. A	2. D	3. D	4. B	5. C	6. D	7. C
8. A	9. D	10. A	11. B	12. C	13. D	14. B
15. D	16. A	17. B	18. C	19. D	20. A	21. C
22. B	23. A	24. C	25. D	26. B	27. C	28. B
29. A	30. A	31. D	32. A	33. B	34. D	35. C

二、简答题

36. **答案要点**：

（1）帝国主义和中华民族的矛盾、封建主义和人民大众的矛盾，是近代中国社会的主要矛盾。其中帝国主义和中华民族的矛盾，是各种矛盾中最主要的矛盾。

（2）近代中国人民面对两大历史任务，一是求得民族独立和人民解放；二是实现国家富强和人民幸福。

37. **答案要点**：

（1）计划经济和市场经济不是划分社会制度的标志，计划经济不等于社会主义，市场经济也不等于资本主义。

（2）计划和市场都是经济手段，对经济活动的调节各有优劣，社会主义实行市场经济要把两者优势结合起来。

（3）市场经济作为资源配置的一种方式，本身不具有制度属性，可以和不同的社会制度结合，从而表现出不同的性质。

38. **答案要点：**

科学发展观，第一要义是发展，核心立场是以人为本，基本要求是全面协调可持续，根本方法是统筹兼顾。

39. **答案要点：**

（1）这是由科学社会主义的理论逻辑所决定的。

（2）这是由中国特色社会主义产生与发展的历史逻辑所决定的。

（3）这是由中国特色社会主义迈向新征程的实践逻辑所决定的。

三、论述题

40. **答案要点：**

（1）感性认识是人们在实践基础上，由感觉器官直接感受到的关于事物的现象、事物的外部联系、事物的各个方面的认识。理性认识是人们借助抽象思维，在概括整理大量感性材料的基础上，达到关于事物的本质、全体、内部联系和事物自身规律性的认识。

（2）感性认识和理性认识的辩证关系：理性认识依赖于感性认识；感性认识有待于发展和深化为理性认识；感性认识和理性认识相互渗透、相互包含。

（3）割裂二者的辩证统一关系，要么走向唯理论，即轻视感性认识而片面夸大理性认识的作用，导致实际工作中犯教条主义的错误；要么走向经验论，即轻视理性认识而片面夸大感性认识的作用，导致实际工作中犯经验主义的错误。

41. **答案要点：**

（1）坚持把国家和民族的发展放在自己力量的基点上，坚定不移走自己的路，走和平发展道路，同时，决不能放弃我们的正当利益，决不能牺牲国家核心利益。

（2）把国家主权和安全放在第一位，坚定地维护我国的国家利益，反对任何国家损害我国的独立、主权、安全和尊严。

（3）从我国人民和世界人民的共同利益出发，对于一切国际事务，都要根据事情本身的是非曲直决定自己的立场和政策，不屈从于任何外来压力。

(4) 坚持各国的事务应由本国政府和人民决定，世界上的事情应由各国政府和人民平等协商，反对一切形式的霸权主义和强权政治。

(5) 主张和平解决国际争端和热点问题，反对动辄诉诸武力或以武力相威胁，反对颠覆别国合法政权，反对一切形式的恐怖主义。

英　　语

总　要　求

考生应掌握基本的英语语言基础知识并具备一定的语言运用能力，包括基本的语音、语法和词汇知识，一定的阅读理解、口语交际以及初步的写作能力。

考试内容

一、语音

考生应掌握下列语音规则：

1. 元音字母在单词中的读音
2. 辅音字母在单词中的读音
3. 常见字母组合的读音

二、词汇

考生应掌握约 3 800 个英语单词，参见后附词汇表。

词汇表仅包含单词的基本词形，未包含单词的读音、词性、意义和形态变化，考生应学习掌握这些内容。同时，考生还应掌握一定的常用短语、习惯用语和搭配用法，掌握单词之间的语义关系，如同义关系、反义关系等。能够根据上下文或利用构词法知识推断语篇中生词的含义。

三、语法

考生应掌握下列基本语法规则：

（一）词法

1. 名词
2. 冠词
3. 代词
4. 数词
5. 形容词
6. 副词
7. 介词
8. 动词
9. 连词
10. 感叹词

（二）句法

1. 基本句型
2. 句子按用途分类

（1）陈述句

（2）疑问句

（3）祈使句

（4）感叹句

3. 句子按结构分类

（1）简单句

（2）并列句

（3）复合句

（三）构词法

1. 派生法
2. 合成法
3. 转换法

四、阅读

考生应能读懂各种题材(包括社会生活、人物传记、科普、史地、政经、文化等)和体裁(包括记叙文、说明文、议论文、应用文等)、生词量不超过所读材料 2%的文字材料。考生应能理解所读材料的主旨大意,掌握主要事实和有关细节,辨识作者的基本态度和观点,能根据有关信息进行一定的推理、判断或引申。

五、写作

考生应能理解所给出的语言情景,能够运用相关的语言知识完成所规定的写作任务。

考试形式及试卷结构

试卷总分:150 分

考试时间:150 分钟

考试方式:闭卷,笔试

考试内容和要求:

第一部分:语音

共 5 个小题,每小题 1 分,共 5 分。要求从所给的四个单词的画线部分中选出一个与其他三个读音不同的选项。

第二部分:语法与词汇

共 15 个小题,每小题 1 分,共 15 分。每小题留有空白处,要求考生从所给的四个选项中选出一个最佳答案填入空白处,使句子符合语法规则,意思完整。

第三部分:完形填空

共 15 个小题,每小题 2 分,共 30 分。该部分是一篇 200 词左右的短文,短文中有 15 处空白,每个空白为 1 小题。每小题有四个选项,要求考生在阅读理解文章内容的基础上,选择一个最佳答案,使短文的意思和结构合理、完整。

第四部分：阅读理解

共20个小题，每小题3分，共60分。该部分由5篇文章组成，阅读量为1 500词左右。每篇文章后有若干小题，要求考生在理解全文的基础上，从题后给出的四个选项中选出一个最符合题意的答案。

第五部分：补全对话

共5个小题，每小题3分，共15分。该部分为一段对话，要求考生在理解对话的基础上，运用所掌握的语言知识，补全对话内容。

第六部分：短文写作

1个小题，25分。该部分要求考生根据所给题目或要求写出一篇100～120词的短文。

以上内容总结为：

部　分	考试内容	题　量	分　值
一	语音	5	5
二	语法与词汇	15	15
三	完形填空	15	30
四	阅读理解	20	60
五	补全对话	5	15
六	短文写作	1	25
总　计		61	150

样　题

Ⅰ. Phonetics (5 points)

Directions: In each of the following groups of words, there are four underlined letters or letter combinations marked A, B, C and D. Compare the underlined parts and identify the one that is different from the others in pronunciation. Mark your answer by blackening the

corresponding letter on the Answer Sheet.

1. A. bear B. pear C. fear D. wear
2. A. case B. base C. ease D. chase
3. A. post B. cost C. most D. host
4. A. scene B. scare C. score D. scale
5. A. mouse B. shout C. cloud D. tough

Ⅱ. Vocabulary and Structure (15 points)

Directions: There are 15 incomplete sentences in this section. For each sentence there are four choices marked A, B, C and D. Choose one answer that best completes the sentence and blacken the corresponding letter on the Answer Sheet.

6. Every time I met her, she would show her concern ________ me and my family.

   A. on B. for C. from D. against

7. Susie's experience is unusual ________ she travelled 20 countries in only one month.

   A. so that B. such that C. in that D. except that

8. By the time he retires, Carl ________ president for 15 years at the university.

   A. will be B. would be

   C. has been D. will have been

9. Natural gas can serve as an ________ to coal and oil because it is more environmentally friendly.

   A. alternative B. extra C. option D. addition

10. Many young people have stopped ________ newspapers because they read the news online now.

    A. buy B. buying C. to buy D. bought

11. —Did you find the film boring?

—Not at all. It was ________.

A. bitter B. horrible C. miserable D. terrific

12. Those ________ are willing to help others are likely to be popular among people.

A. who B. what C. which D. whose

13. The pipe in the kitchen is broken. We should have it ________ as soon as possible.

A. repairing B. repaired

C. to repair D. to be repaired

14. Mary demanded that he ________ the books he borrowed from her a month ago.

A. return B. had returned

C. would return D. returned

15. There are enough night schools in this city. Adults can be educated no matter ________ old they are.

A. what B. where C. how D. when

16. ________ the result of the exam, she stood at the door of the classroom, disappointed.

A. Known B. Knowing

C. To know D. To be known

17. The librarian did some careful checking and found several books ________ from the shelf.

A. dropping B. losing C. missing D. leaking

18. We have to accept the fact ________ there is a shortage of qualified teachers in the countryside.

A. that B. because C. which D. since

19. The company has 80 staff members, ________ 15 foreign experts.

A. not counted B. not to count

C. not counting D. having not counted

20. The young mother ________ ever gets a chance to study, except

when the children have gone to bed.

A.only B. nearly C. almost D. hardly

Ⅲ. Cloze (30 points)

Directions: For each blank in the following passage, there are four choices marked A, B, C and D. Choose the one that is most suitable and mark your answer by blackening the corresponding letter on the Answer Sheet.

As children move towards adulthood (成年), they become taller, stronger, and more independent. At some point in adulthood, __21__, a slow decline begins. Their hair often __22__ grey, their skin wrinkles, and their muscles begin to __23__. Their short-term memory may suffer, and they often __24__ part of their vision or hearing.

Scientists are not __25__ sure what causes the effects of aging. The body might have a time __26__ which would determine how long the cells can remain __27__. Depending on the type of animal and its environment, animals age at different rates and live __28__ different lengths of time. An animal in a good zoo—well __29__ and protected from predators (捕食者)—often lives longer than the same type in the wild. __30__, people who live in rich countries generally live longer than __31__ in poor countries.

Several other factors also __32__ how long people live and the quality of their lives. One factor is genetics (遗传). In some families, it seems that many __33__ have long lives. Genetics may also determine whether people __34__ certain diseases. Another factor is lifestyle. People who keep their minds __35__ and often communicate with friends will feel younger and may live longer. People who keep a normal weight, exercise, and do not smoke may also age more slowly.

21. A. however	B. therefore	C. besides	D. moreover
22. A. stays	B. falls	C. turns	D. seems
23. A. develop	B. fade	C. grow	D. shrink
24. A. lose	B. harm	C. improve	D. protect
25. A. strictly	B. exactly	C. purely	D. simply
26. A. link	B. limit	C. label	D. lack
27. A. bright	B. stable	C. secure	D. healthy
28. A. with	B. for	C. on	D. in
29. A. fed	B. clothed	C. behaved	D. trained
30. A. Commonly	B. Mostly	C. Finally	D. Similarly
31. A. that	B. those	C. some	D. others
32. A. judge	B. cause	C. affect	D. form
33. A. names	B. races	C. friends	D. members
34. A. get	B. take	C. make	D. cause
35. A. clever	B. firm	C. active	D. calm

Ⅳ. Reading Comprehension (60 points)

Directions: There are five reading passages in this part. Each passage is followed by four questions. For each question there are four suggested answers marked A, B, C and D. Choose one best answer and blacken the corresponding letter on the Answer Sheet.

Passage One

Welcome to Stratford-upon-Avon, home of the world's most famous writer, William Shakespeare (1564—1616). Stratford is an ancient town with many old buildings from the Middle Ages. Our aim is to attract you to explore our lovely town following streets that Shakespeare would have known and would still recognize.

Stratford-upon-Avon has been a market town since before Shakespeare's day. It was a small river crossing until it received its legal status as a town in 1196. The original crossing was close to the site of Clopton Bridge, one of the oldest bridges in the country. After 500 years, the bridge still bears traffic, which speaks of the great skill of the original builders. Today, we still have a flourishing market, held on Fridays and Saturdays. The town is also host to many other markets throughout the year.

The Royal Shakespeare Company, one of the most famous acting companies in the world, is located here. The theatre provides performances of Shakespeare's plays. It also performs works from across the centuries and many contemporary pieces as well. If you are lucky, you will see many a famous face wandering through the town or enjoying a drink after plays in one of our many bars.

You may enjoy a boat trip on the river or a visit to the Butterfly Farm, one of the largest of its kind in Europe, which has collections of many extraordinary insects. An enjoyable time may be had in the Brass Rubbing Centre（黄铜拓印技艺中心）, which promises that great skills are not required to produce an unusual souvenir of your visit. The centre of the town has many small shops and galleries. We hope you enjoy your visit to our much-loved town and that you will come back again.

36. What can be inferred about Stratford-upon-Avon?

A. Its market is closed on Saturday mornings.

B. It has served as an art market since Shakespeare's day.

C. It gained its legal status as a town in Shakespeare's day.

D. Its streets have remained nearly the same over the centuries.

37. Which place should you visit if you want to observe wonderful insects?

A. Butterfly Farm. B. Clopton Bridge.

C. Brass Rubbing Centre.   D. Royal Shakespeare Company.

38. What is the main purpose of this passage?

A. To introduce the history of Stratford-upon-Avon.

B. To inform visitors of the places to buy souvenirs.

C. To attract visitors to travel in Stratford-upon-Avon.

D. To associate Stratford-upon-Avon with Shakespeare.

39. Where is the passage most probably taken from?

A. A novel.   B. A biography.

C. A product catalogue.   D. A tourist guide.

Passage Two

Health care experts have long drawn attention to the problems of eating too much salt. There is strong evidence that a diet high in salt can lead to raised blood pressure. Since high blood pressure is a major factor in heart disease, it makes sense to cut down on the salt people eat.

In the past, food contained very little salt, and people added it to their food at the table. Very few people add salt this way nowadays. However, the salt content of processed foods has gone up dramatically. It's now estimated that over three-quarters of the salt in the average diet comes from processed foods, eaten without our being aware of it.

Salt is added to food partly to extend shelf-life, but more often it's dropped in to make up for flavours lost in the manufacturing process. This is especially true of ready meals and highly processed foods, but it's also true of such basic food as biscuits, soups, and even bread. Much mass-produced bread, for instance, contains so much salt—half a gram for every hundred grams of bread—that it's officially classified by the UK government as high-salt food. Salt has to be added to the bread because fast production cuts down the time for flavour to develop. Without added salt, the bread would taste like paper.

In the UK, the government has launched a campaign to cut down on the salt people eat. The UK Food Standards Agency argues that nearly half of the UK's population eat too much salt—9.5g a day on average. Its aim is to bring down the average to 6g a day. The idea is to cut the salt content in 85 key food categories such as bread, meat, and cakes.

40. What is the main reason for reducing salt in food?
    A. To improve the flavour of food.
    B. To extend the shelf-life of food.
    C. To protect people against heart diseases.
    D. To decrease the time for processing food.

41. What can be inferred about people's use of salt in the past?
    A. People ate much salt in their average diet.
    B. People used salt to control blood pressure.
    C. People didn't eat so much salt as we do today.
    D. People were clear about the harmful effect of salt.

42. Which of the following is classified as high-salt food by the UK government?
    A. Sweet biscuits. B. Fresh vegetables.
    C. Light-cooked meat. D. Mass-produced bread.

43. What is the passage mainly about?
    A. Salt and people's health. B. Salt and food flavour.
    C. Salt and food processing. D. Salt and people's lifestyle.

Passage Three

Music is part of the structure of our society; it sits at the heart of human experience and enriches (丰富) so many lives. Why, then, is it not central to our education system? This is a question I recently put forward to an all-party group on music education.

I am 20 years old and began playing saxophone, aged 7, at the Barracudas Band in Barrow-in-Furness. The funding for the centre has now been cut. I took part in the primary tuition project, aged 11. The funding for that has also been cut now. It is a common problem across the country.

Music is not an add-on, a "soft" subject or a luxury—it is absolutely essential to our existence. Every child deserves the opportunity to experience its benefits. Until music is held in the same regard as the "core" subjects of our curriculum, our society will be worse off. We need joy, empathy (共情) and hope on this planet more than ever, and taking away children's opportunity to develop musical skills is to set ourselves up for a fall. Despite the many brilliant programs and projects to encourage young musicians ("Every Child a Musician," "Awards for Young Musicians," to name but a few), we are reaching a crisis point. We are in danger of destroying creativity, innovation (创新) and expression. Learning an instrument can help develop so many fundamental life skills. It promotes discipline, empathy, determination and cooperation as well as providing a sense of community and worth.

Music has changed my life. It is a huge part of who I am. I have learned so much about the world through music and the inspiring figures I have met through it. I feel I have a duty to help ensure that others can benefit from its magic. Let us make it available to every single child.

44. Why did the author raise the question on music education?

A. The tuition fee for music training has risen.

B. The band the author joined has broken up.

C. The project the author was in no longer exists.

D. The funding for music education has been cut.

45. What does the author think of the role of music?

A. It can help children learn core subjects.

B. It is fundamental to the growth of a child.

C. It is important for dealing with social crises.

D. It may offer children future job opportunities.

46. What is the theme of the passage?

A. Music training programs should be provided free.

B. Music should be made popular across the country.

C. Music education should be available to every child.

D. Music should be placed at the top of the curriculum.

47. What is the author's attitude towards music?

A. Positive. B. Indifferent. C. Critical. D. Doubtful.

Passage Four

In 2011, a dog owner named Robert uploaded a video titled "Guilty!" to YouTube. He had come home finding his two dogs near an empty bag of cat treats. The first dog behaved calmly. But the second dog, Denver, sat shaking in a corner, her eyes looking down, which made Robert believe it was she who had done it. Seeing her "apparent admission of guilt," he yelled at her. "You did this!" Denver beat her tail nervously. "You know the routine. In the kennel (狗窝)!" Following the command, the dog shut herself in.

The video quickly gathered a flood of comments. Since then, "dog shaming" has become popular on the Internet, as owners around the world posted beside notes shots of their trembling pets in which the dogs seemed to admit bad behavior. For instance, "I ate an extra large pizza," admits a chocolate Lab. Human enthusiasm for guilty dogs seemed growing.

But according to a researcher at Barnard College, what we consider to be a dog's guilty look is no sign of guilt at all. In a 2009 study, the researcher had owners forbid their dogs from eating an attractive treat, and then asked the owners to leave the room. While each owner was gone, the researcher either removed the treat or fed it to the dog. When the owners returned, they were told—regardless of the truth—that their dogs either had or had not eaten it. If owners thought their dogs had done something wrong, blames followed, and guilty looks quickly emerged. Yet dogs who hadn't eaten the treat were more likely to appear guilty than dogs who had—so long as their owners scolded them. Far from signaling regret, one group of researchers wrote in a 2012 paper, the guilty look of dogs is very likely a means to show obedience (顺从) to their owners.

48. What did Robert want to show with his video on YouTube?
   A. Dogs' naughty behaviors.
   B. Dogs' trust in their owners.
   C. Dogs' apparent guilty looks.
   D. Dogs' conflict with other pets.

49. How did people react to Robert's video?
   A. They began to blame their own dogs.
   B. They began to read stories about dogs.
   C. They started to share dog-shaming photos.
   D. They started to show sympathy for his dog.

50. What does "a chocolate Lab" in Paragraph 2 refer to?
   A. A dog. B. A cat.
   C. A scientist. D. A researcher.

51. Why do dogs wear a guilty look according to the researchers?
   A. To deceive their owners.
   B. To beg their owners for treats.
   C. To attract their owners' attention.
   D. To show obedience to their owners.

Passage Five

Pain is an emotional as well as physical response to injury or disease. Intense fear and anxiety are vital immediate responses that cause you to avoid sources of pain whenever possible. Sometimes, however, pain persists even when the injury or disease is no longer present. A painful feeling can become associated with constant stress, bad memories, or lasting fear.

Medicine is often essential for controlling pain in the short term, but taking painkillers（止痛药）for an extended period can lead to addiction（上瘾）or serious physical side effects, including stomach and liver diseases. Your body may also build up a tolerance to a drug so that you get less benefit from it as time goes on.

Although you should always seek medical advice if pain is severe or continues for a long time, you can also use techniques to control it. Mind-body techniques can reduce or help control pain—with no risk of side effects. Most people relax with deep, controlled breathing to reduce the tension that comes with pain. Try lying quietly in a dark room; breathe in deeply while counting to 10, hold the breath for a moment, and then exhale slowly for a count of 10. Continue this for 10—20 minutes.

Shifting your attention often reduces pain's severity（严重程度）. Try turning your attention away from the painful area, focusing instead on a non-painful part of your body. Or, imagine the pain as a big ball of energy outside your body, and make it smaller in your mind. Train yourself to replace the thoughts like "I can't stop this pain," with positive ones such as "This pain is only temporary."

In this practice, you merely acknowledge the pain by actively fighting it, instead of allowing it to dominate your thoughts.

52. Which of the following is people's natural response to pain?

A. They prefer to forget the bad memories.

B. They tend to feel worried and frightened.

C. They try to find out what may cause pain.

D. They want to make sure it won't last long.

53. What can be inferred about taking painkillers from Paragraph 2?

A. It builds up the tolerance to pain.

B. It becomes less effective over time.

C. It cures stomach and liver diseases slowly.

D. It leads to addiction in a short period of time.

54. Which of the following is closest in meaning to the word "exhale" in Paragraph 3?

A. To get up.　　B. To fall asleep.

C. To breathe out.　　D. To turn your body.

55. What would be the best title for the passage?

A. How to Use Your Brain to Manage Pain?

B. How to Eliminate Painkillers' Side Effects?

C. What Is the Correct Way to Take Medicines?

D. What Is the Right Way to Shift Your Attention?

Ⅴ. Daily Conversation (15 points)

Directions: Pick out appropriate expressions from the eight choices below and complete the following dialogue by blackening the corresponding letter on the Answer Sheet.

A. No, thanks.	B. Would you like to join us?
C. That is a lovely place.	D. When shall we leave?
E. See you then!	F. I am free on Sunday.
G. I need a break!	H. Where are you planning to go?

Daniel：How are you doing，Linda?

Linda：To be honest，I am really tired of my work at the moment. ___56___

Daniel：My friends and I are planning a trip on Sunday. ___57___

Linda：Sure，I'd love to. ___58___

Daniel：The Golden Beach. We will have a picnic there. It will be fun!

Linda：I can't wait! ___59___

Daniel：Eight o'clock in the morning. We'll pick you up at your place.

Linda：Great! ___60___

Ⅵ. Writing (25 points)

Directions：For this part，you are supposed to write an e-mail of 100—120 words based on the following situation. Remember to write it clearly on the Answer Sheet.

61. 学校将组织一次英语演讲比赛，打算邀请外教(John)来做评委。请你(Li Yuan)给他写一封电子邮件(e-mail)，内容包括：

- 邀请他担任评委(judge)；
- 告知他比赛安排(如：时间、地点等)；
- 希望他赛后进行点评；
- 期待他能接受邀请。

参考答案

Ⅰ. Phonetics

1. C　　2. C　　3. B　　4. A　　5. D

Ⅱ. Vocabulary and Structure

6. B　　7. C　　8. D　　9. A　　10. B

11. D　　12. A　　13. B　　14. A　　15. C

16. B	17. C	18. A	19. C	20. D

Ⅲ. Cloze

21. A	22. C	23. D	24. A	25. B
26. B	27. D	28. B	29. A	30. D
31. B	32. C	33. D	34. A	35. C

Ⅳ. Reading Comprehension

36. D	37. A	38. C	39. D	40. C
41. C	42. D	43. A	44. D	45. B
46. C	47. A	48. C	49. C	50. A
51. D	52. B	53. B	54. C	55. A

Ⅴ. Daily Conversation

56. G	57. B	58. H	59. D	60. E

Ⅵ. Writing

61.（略）

附录

词　汇　表

a / an
abandon
ability
able
abnormal
aboard
abolish
about
above
abroad
abrupt
absence
absent
absolute
absorb
abstract
abundant
abuse
academic
academy
accelerate
accent
accept
access
accident
accommodation / accommodations
accompany
accomplish
according to
account
accountant
accumulate
accurate
accuse
ache
achieve
achievement
acid

acknowledge
acquaintance
acquire
acre
across
act
action
active
activity
actor / actress
actual
AD / A.D.
adapt
add
addict
addition
additional
address
adequate
adjust
administration
admire
admission
admit
adopt
adorable
adult
advance
advantage
adventure
advertise
advertisement / ad
advice
advise
advocate
aeroplane / airplane
affair
affect
affection
afford
afraid
after
afternoon
afterwards / afterward
again
against
age
agency
agenda
agent
aggressive
ago
agree
agreement
agriculture
ahead
aid
aim
air
aircraft

airline
airport
alarm
album
alcohol
alcoholic
alert
alike
alive
all
alley
allow
almost
alone
along
alongside
aloud
alphabet
already
also
alter
alternative
although
altitude
altogether
always
a.m. / A.M.
amateur
amaze
amazing
ambassador
ambition
ambulance
among / amongst
amount
amuse
amusement
analyse / analyze
analysis
ancestor
ancient
and
anger
angle
angry
animal
ankle
anniversary
announce
annoy
annual
another
answer
ant
anticipate
antique
anxiety
anxious
any
anybody / anyone

anyhow
anything
anyway
anywhere
apart
apartment
apologise / apologize
apology
apparent
appeal
appear
appearance
appetite
applaud
apple
applicant
application
apply
appoint
appointment
appreciate
approach
appropriate
approval
approve
approximate
April
arch
architect
architecture
area
argue
argument
arise
arm
army
around
arouse
arrange
arrangement
arrest
arrival
arrive
arrow
art
article
artificial
artist
as
ash
ashamed
aside
ask
asleep
aspect
assemble
assess
assessment
assign
assist

assistance
assistant
associate
association
assume
assure
astonish
astronaut
astronomer
astronomy
at
athlete
athletic
atmosphere
atom
attach
attack
attain
attempt
attend
attention
attitude
attract
attraction
attractive
attribute
audience
August
aunt
author
authority
automatic
automobile / auto
autonomous
autumn / fall
available
avenue
average
avoid
awake
award
aware
away
awesome
awful
awkward
baby
bachelor
back
background
backward
bacon
bacteria
bad
badly
badminton
bag
baggage
bake
bakery

balance
balcony
ball
ballet
balloon
bamboo
ban
banana
band
bank
bankrupt
banquet
bar
barbecue
barber
bare
barely
bargain
bark
barrier
base
baseball
basement
basic
basin
basis
basket
basketball
bat
bath
bathe
bathroom
battery
battle
bay
BC / B.C.
be
beach
beam
bean
bear
beard
beast
beat
beautiful
beauty
because
become
bed
bedroom
bee
beef
beer
before
beforehand
beg
beggar
begin
behalf
behave

behaviour / behavior
behind
being
belief
believe
bell
belly
belong
below
belt
bench
bend
beneath
beneficial
benefit
beside
besides
best
bet
betray
better
between
beverage
beyond
bias
bicycle / bike
bid
big
bill
billion
biography
biology
bird
birth
birthday
biscuit
bit
bite
bitter
black
blackboard
blame
blank
blanket
bleed
blend
bless
blind
block
blood
bloom
blouse
blow
blue
board
boast
boat
body
boil
bold

bomb
bond
bone
bonus
book
boom
boost
boot
booth
border
bored
boring
born
borrow
boss
botany
both
bother
bottle
bottom
bounce
bound
boundary
bow
bowl
bowling
box
boxing
boy
brain
brake
branch
brand
brave
bravery
bread
break
breakfast
breakthrough
breast
breath
breathe
brick
bride
bridegroom
bridge
brief
bright
brilliant
bring
broad
broadcast
brochure
broom
brother
brown
brush
budget
buffet
build

building
bull
bunch
bundle
burden
burglar
burn
burst
bury
bus
bush
business
businessman / businesswoman
busy
but
butcher
butter
butterfly
button
buy
by
cab
cabbage
cabinet
cable
cafe / café
cafeteria
cage
cake
calculate
calendar
call
calligraphy
calm
calorie
camel
camera
camp
campaign
campus
can
canal
cancel
cancer
candidate
candle
candy
canteen
cap
capable
capacity
capital
capsule
captain
caption
capture
car
carbon
card
care

career
careful
careless
carpet
carriage
carrier
carrot
carry
cartoon
carve
case
cash
cast
castle
casual
cat
catalogue / catalog
catch
category
cattle
cause
caution
cautious
cave
cease
ceiling
celebrate
celebration
celebrity
cell
cent
centigrade / Celsius
centimetre / centimeter
central
centre / center
century
ceremony
certain
certainly
certificate
chain
chair
chairman / chairwoman / chairperson
chalk
challenge
challenging
champion
chance
change
channel
chaos
chapter
character
characteristic
charge
charity
chart
chase
chat
cheap

cheat
check
cheek
cheer
cheerful
cheese
chef
chemical
chemist
chemistry
cheque / check
chess
chest
chew
chicken
chief
child
childhood
chin
china
chocolate
choice
choke
choose
chopsticks
chorus
Christmas
church
cigar
cigarette / cigaret
cinema
circle
circuit
circulate
circumstance
circus
cite
citizen
city
civil
civilian
civilisation / civilization
claim
clap
clarify
class
classic
classify
classmate
classroom
clay
clean
cleaner
clear
clerk
clever
click
client
climate
climb

clinic
clock
clone
close
cloth
clothes
clothing
cloud
cloudy
club
clue
clumsy
coach
coal
coarse
coast
coat
cock
coffee
coin
coincidence
cold
collapse
collar
colleague
collect
collection
collective
college
collide
collision
colour / color
column
comb
combination
combine
come
comedy
comfort
comfortable
comic
command
comment
commerce
commercial
commit
committee
common
communicate
communication
communism
communist
community
companion
company
comparative
compare
compass
compete
competence

competition
complain
complete
complex
complicated
component
compose
composition
comprehension
comprehensive
comprise
compromise
compulsory
computer
concentrate
concept
concern
concert
conclude
conclusion
concrete
condemn
condition
conduct
conductor
conference
confident
confirm
conflict
confuse
congratulate
congratulation
congress
connect
conquer
conscience
conscious
consequence
consequently
conservation
conservative
consider
considerable
considerate
consideration
consist
consistent
constant
constitution
construct
construction
consult
consume
contact
contain
container
contemporary
content
contest
context

continent
continual
continue
continuous
contract
contradict
contradiction
contradictory
contrary
contrast
contribute
contribution
control
controversial
convenience
convenient
conventional
conversation
convey
convince
cook
cooker
cookie
cool
cooperate
cope
copy
core
corn
corner
corporate
corporation
correct
correction
correspond
corresponding
corridor
corrupt
cost
costume
cottage
cotton
cough
could
council
count
counter
country
countryside
county
couple
courage
course
court
courtyard
cousin
cover
coverage
cow
crash

crayon
crazy
cream
create
creative
creature
credit
crew
crime
criminal
crisis
criterion
critic
critical
criticise / criticize
criticism
crop
cross
crossroads
crowd
crucial
crude
cruel
crush
cry
crystal
cube
cucumber
cuisine
cultivate
culture
cup
cupboard
cure
curiosity
curious
currency
current
curriculum
curse
curtain
cushion
custom
customer
cut
cute
cycle
cyclist
daily
dairy
dam
damage
damp
dance
danger
dangerous
dare
dark
dash
data

database
date
daughter
dawn
day
dead
deadline
deaf
deal
dear
death
debate
debt
decade
decay
deceive
December
decent
decide
decision
declare
decline
decorate
decoration
decrease
deed
deep
deer
defeat
defence / defense
defend
define
definite
degree
delay
delete
deliberately
delicate
delicious
delight
deliver
delivery
demand
democracy
demonstrate
dense
dentist
deny
depart
department
departure
depend
dependent
deposit
depress
depth
derive
describe
description
desert

deserve
design
desirable
desire
desk
despair
desperate
despite
dessert
destination
destroy
destruction
detail
detect
detective
determine
develop
development
device
devil
devote
diagram
dial
dialect
dialogue / dialog
diamond
diary
dictionary
die
diet
differ
difference
different
difficult
difficulty
dig
digest
digital
dignity
dilemma
dimension
dining
dinner
dinosaur
dip
diploma
direct
direction
director
directory
dirt
dirty
disabled
disadvantage
disagree
disappear
disappoint
disappointed
disaster
disc / disk

discipline
discount
discourage
discover
discovery
discrimination
discuss
discussion
disease
dish
dislike
dismiss
disorder
display
dispute
distance
distant
distinction
distinguish
distress
distribute
district
disturb
disturbing
dive
diverse
divide
division
divorce
dizzy
do
doctor / Dr / Dr.
document
dog
doll
dollar
domain
domestic
dominate
donate
door
dormitory / dorm
dot
double
doubt
doubtful
down
download
downstairs
downtown
dozen
draft
drag
drama
dramatic
draw
drawer
dream
dress
drill

drink
drive
driver
drop
drought
drug
drum
drunk
dry
duck
due
dull
dumb
dumpling
duration
during
dusk
dust
dustbin
duty
dynamic
dynasty
each
eager
eagle
ear
early
earn
earth
earthquake
ease
east
eastern
easy
eat
echo
ecology
economic
economical
economy
edge
edition
editor
educate
education
educator
effect
effective
efficient
effort
egg
eight
eighteen
eighth
eighty
either
elder
elderly
elect
election

electric
electrical
electricity
electronic
elegant
element
elementary
elephant
elevator
eleven
eliminate
else
elsewhere
email / e-mail
embarrass
embassy
emerge
emergency
emigrate
emotion
emperor
emphasis
emphasise / emphasize
empire
employ
employee
employer
empty
enable
enclose
encounter
encourage
encouragement
end
ending
endless
endure
enemy
energetic
energy
engage
engine
engineer
engineering
enhance
enjoy
enjoyable
enlarge
enormous
enough
enquire / inquire
enrol / enroll
ensure
enter
enterprise
entertain
entertainment
enthusiasm
enthusiastic
entire

entitle
entrance
entry
envelope
environment
envy
episode
equal
equality
equator
equip
equipment
era
erase
eraser
error
erupt
escalator
escape
especially
essay
essential
establish
estate
estimate
evaluate
eve
even
evening
event
eventually
ever
every
everybody / everyone
everyday
everything
everywhere
evidence
evident
evil
evolution
exact
examination / exam
examine
example
exceed
excellent
except
exception
excess
exchange
excite
exciting
excuse
execute
executive
exercise
exhibition
exist
existence

exit
expand
expect
expectation
expense
expensive
experience
experiment
expert
explain
explanation
explicit
explode
exploit
explore
export
expose
express
expression
extend
extension
extensive
extent
external
extinction
extra
extraordinary
extreme
eye
eyesight

fabric
face
facial
facilitate
facility
fact
factor
factory
faculty
fade
fail
failure
faint
fair
faith
faithful
fake
fall
false
fame
familiar
family
famous
fan
fancy
fantastic
fantasy
far
fare
farewell

farm
farmer
farther
fashion
fast
fasten
fat
fate
father / dad
fault
favour / favor
favourable / favorable
favourite / favorite
fax
fear
feast
feather
feature
February
federal
fee
feed
feel
feeling
fellow
female
fence
ferry
fertiliser / fertilizer
festival
fetch
fever
few
fibre / fiber
fiction
field
fierce
fifteen
fifth
fifty
fight
figure
file
fill
film
final
finance
financial
find
fine
finger
finish
fire
fireworks
firm
first
fish
fisherman
fist
fit

five
fix
flag
flame
flash
flashlight
flat
flavour / flavor
flee
flesh
flexible
flight
float
flood
floor
flour
flourish
flow
flower
flu
fluency
fluent
fluid
fly
focus
fog
foggy
fold
folk
follow
fond
food
fool
foolish
foot
football
for
forbid
force
forecast
forehead
foreign
foreigner
foresee
forest
forever
forget
forgive
fork
form
formal
format
former
forth
fortnight
fortunate
fortune
forty
forward
found

fountain
four
fourteen
fox
fragrant
framework
frank
free
freedom
freeway
freeze
freezing
frequency
frequent
fresh
friction
Friday
friend
friendly
friendship
frighten
frog
from
front
frontier
frost
fruit
fry
fuel
fulfil / fulfill
full
fun
function
fund
fundamental
funeral
funny
fur
furnish
furniture
further
furthermore
future
gain
gallery
gallon
gamble
game
gap
garage
garbage
garden
garlic
gas
gate
gather
gay
gender
gene
general

generally
generate
generation
generator
generous
gentle
gentleman
genuine
geography
geometry
gesture
get
ghost
giant
gift
gifted
giraffe
girl
give
glad
glance
glass
glimpse
global
globe
glory
glove
glue
go
goal
goat
god
gold
golden
golf
good
goodbye / bye
goose
govern
government
governor
grab
graceful
grade
gradual
gradually
graduate
graduation
grain
grammar
gramme / gram
grand
grandfather / grandpa
grandmother / grandma / granny
grandson
grape
graph
grasp
grass
grateful

gratitude
gravity
great
greedy
green
greenhouse
greet
greeting
grey / gray
grief
grocery
ground
group
grow
growth
guarantee
guard
guess
guest
guidance
guide
guideline
guilty
guitar
gun
guy
gymnasium / gym
gymnastics
habit
habitat
hair
haircut
half
hall
halt
ham
hamburger / burger
hammer
hand
handbag
handful
handicap
handkerchief
handle
handsome
handwriting
handy
hang
happen
happiness
happy
harbour / harbor
hard
hardly
hardware
harm
harmful
harmony
harvest
haste

hat
hatch
hate
have
he
head
headache
headline
headmaster / headmistress
headquarters
health
healthy
hear
heart
heat
heaven
heavy
heel
height
helicopter
hell
hello
help
helpful
hen
hence
her
herb
herd
here
hero / heroine
hers
herself
hesitate
hi / hey
hide
high
highlight
highway
hike
hill
him
himself
hint
hire
his
history
hit
hobby
hold
hole
holiday
holy
home
homeland
hometown
homework
honest
honey
honour / honor

honourable / honorable
hook
hope
hopeful
hopeless
horrible
horror
horse
hospital
host / hostess
hostile
hot
hotdog
hotel
hour
house
household
housewife
housework
how
however
hug
huge
human
humble
humid
humorous
humour / humor
hundred
hunger
hungry
hunt
hunter
hurricane
hurry
hurt
husband
hydrogen
hygiene
I
ice
ice cream
idea
ideal
identical
identify
identity
idiom
idle
if
ignore
ill
illegal
illness
illustrate
image
imaginary
imagine
imitate
immediate

immigrant
impact
implication
imply
import
importance
important
impossible
impress
impression
improve
improvement
in
inch
incident
include
income
increase
incredible
indeed
independence
independent
indicate
indifferent
individual
indoors
industrial
industry
inevitable
infection
infer
influence
inform
information
inherit
initial
initiative
injure
injury
ink
inn
inner
innocent
innovation
input
insect
insert
inside
insight
insist
inspect
inspire
install
instance
instant
instead
institute
institution
instruct
instruction

instrument
insult
insurance
insure
integrate
integrity
intelligence
intelligent
intend
intense
intensive
intention
interaction
interest
interesting
internal
international
Internet / internet
interpret
interrupt
interval
intervention
interview
into
introduce
introduction
invade
invalid
invaluable
invent
invest
investigate
invisible
invitation
invite
involve
iron
island
isolate
issue
it
item
its
itself
jacket
jam
January
jar
jaw
jazz
jealous
jeans
jeep
jet
jewel
job
jog
join
joint
joke

journal
journalist
journey
joy
judge
judgement / judgment
juice
July
jump
June
jungle
junior
just
justice
justify
kangaroo
keep
kettle
key
keyboard
kick
kid
kidnap
kill
kilogramme / kilogram / kilo
kilometre / kilometer
kind
kindergarten
kindness
king
kingdom
kiss
kit
kitchen
kite
knee
knife
knit
knock
know
knowledge
label
laboratory / lab
labour / labor
lack
ladder
lady
lake
lamb
lame
lamp
land
landlord / landlady
landscape
language
lantern
lap
laptop
large
last

late
later
Latin
latter
laugh
laughter
launch
laundry
law
lawn
lawyer
lay
layer
lazy
lead
leader
leadership
leaf
league
leak
lean
learn
least
leather
leave
lecture
left
leg
legal
legend
leisure
lemon
lemonade
lend
length
less
lesson
let
letter
level
liable
liberate
liberation
liberty
librarian
library
licence / license
lid
lie
life
lift
light
lightening
like
likely
limit
line
link
lion
lip

liquid
list
listen
literally
literary
literature
litre / liter
litter
little
live
lively
liver
load
loaf
loan
local
locate
location
lock
log
logic
logical
lonely
long
look
loose
lorry
lose
loss
lot
loud
lounge
love
lovely
low
lower
loyal
luck
lucky
luggage
lunar
lunch
lung
luxury
machine
mad
madam
magazine
magic
magnificent
maid
mail
main
mainland
maintain
major
majority
make
male
man

manage
manager
mankind
manner
manufacture
many
map
marathon
marble
March
march
mark
market
marriage
marry
marvellous / marvelous
mask
mass
massive
master
mat
match
material
mathematics / maths / math
matter
mature
maximum
May
may
maybe
mayor
me
meal
mean
meaning
means
meanwhile
measure
meat
mechanic
medal
media
medical
medicine
medium
meet
meeting
melon
melt
member
membership
memorial
memory
mental
mention
menu
merchant
mercy
merely
merit

merry
mess
message
messy
metal
method
metre / meter
microscope
microwave
middle
midnight
might
migrate
mild
mile
military
milk
millimetre / millimeter
million
millionaire
mind
mine
mineral
minibus
minimum
minister
ministry
minor
minority
minus
minute
miracle
mirror
misery
mislead
Miss
miss
missile
missing
mission
mist
mistake
mistaken
misunderstand
mix
mixture
mobile
mode
model
modern
modest
moment
Monday
money
monitor
monkey
month
monthly
monument
mood

moon
mop
moral
more
moreover
morning
mosquito
most
mostly
mother / mum / mom
motion
motivate
motivation
motive
motor
motorcycle
motto
mount
mountain
mouse
mouth
move
movement
movie
Mr / Mr.
Mrs / Mrs.
Ms / Ms.
much
mud
muddy
multiple
multiply
murder
muscle
museum
mushroom
music
musician
must
my
myself
mysterious
mystery
nail
naked
name
narrow
nation
national
nationality
nationwide
native
natural
nature
naughty
navy
near
nearby
nearly
neat

necessary
neck
necklace
need
needle
negative
neglect
negotiate
neighbour / neighbor
neighbourhood / neighborhood
neither
nephew
nervous
nest
net
network
never
nevertheless
new
news
newspaper
next
nice
niece
night
nightmare
nine
nineteen
ninety
ninth
no
noble
nobody
nod
noise
noisy
none
nonsense
noodle
noon
nor
normal
north
northern
nose
not
note
notebook
nothing
notice
novel
novelist
November
now
nowadays
nowhere
nuclear
numb
number / No.
numerous

nurse
nursery
nut
nutrition
nutritious
o'clock
obey
object
objective
obligation
observe
obstacle
obtain
obvious
occasion
occupation
occupy
occur
ocean
October
odd
of
off
offence / offense
offend
offensive
offer
office
officer
official
offshore
often
oil
OK / okay
old
Olympic
omit
on
once
one
oneself
onion
online
only
onto
open
opening
opera
operate
operation
operator
opinion
opponent
opportunity
oppose
opposite
optimistic
option
optional
or

oral
orange
orbit
order
ordinary
organ
organic
organisation / organization
organise / organize
origin
original
originate
orphan
other
otherwise
ought to
our
ours
ourselves
out
outbreak
outcome
outdoor
outer
outgoing
outing
outline
outlook
output
outside
outstanding
over
overall
overcoat
overcome
overhead
overlook
overseas
overweight
overwhelm
owe
owing to
own
owner
ownership
ox
oxygen
pace
pack
package
packet
page
pain
painful
paint
painter
painting
pair
palace
pale

palm
pan
pancake
panda
panel
panic
paper
paperwork
parade
paragraph
parallel
parcel
pardon
parent
park
parking
part
part-time
partial
participate
particular
partly
partner
party
pass
passage
passenger
passerby
passion
passive
passport
past
paste
patent
path
patience
patient
patriotic
pattern
pause
pave
pavement
pay
payment
pea
peace
peaceful
peach
peak
pear
pearl
peculiar
pedestrian
pen
penalty
pencil
penny
pension
people
pepper

per
perceive
percent / per cent
percentage
perfect
perform
performance
performer
perfume
perhaps
period
permanent
permission
permit
persist
person
personal
personality
personnel
persuade
pessimistic
pest
pet
petrol / gasoline / gasolene
phase
phenomenon
philosophy
phone
photocopy
photograph / photo
phrase
physical
physician
physicist
physics
pianist
piano
pick
picnic
picture
pie
piece
pig
pigeon
pile
pill
pillar
pillow
pilot
pin
pine
pineapple
pink
pint
pioneer
pipe
pitch
pity
place
plain

plan
plane
planet
plant
plastic
plate
platform
play
playground
pleasant
please
pleased
pleasure
plentiful
plenty
plot
plug
plus
p.m. / P.M.
pocket
poem
poet
poetry
point
poison
poisonous
polar
pole
police
policeman / policewoman
policy
polish
polite
political
politician
politics
pollute
pollution
pond
pool
poor
popcorn
popular / pop
popularity
population
pork
porridge
port
portable
porter
pose
position
positive
possess
possession
possibility
possible
post
postage
postcard

postcode
poster
postgraduate
postman / mailman
postpone
pot
potato
potential
pound
pour
poverty
powder
power
powerful
practical
practice
practise
praise
pray
prayer
precious
precise
predict
prefer
preference
pregnant
prejudice
premier
preparation
prepare
prescription
presence
present
presentation
preserve
president
press
pressure
pretend
pretty
prevent
previous
price
pride
primary
prime
primitive
prince
princess
principal
principle
print
prior
priority
prison
prisoner
privacy
private
privilege
prize

probably
problem
procedure
proceed
process
procession
produce
product
production
profession
professional
professor
profile
profit
profound
programme / program
progress
progressive
prohibit
project
promise
promote
promotion
pronounce
pronunciation
proof
proper
property
proportion
proposal
prospect
protect
protein
protest
proud
prove
provide
province
psychological
psychology
pub
public
publish
pull
pulse
pump
punctual
punctuation
punish
punishment
pupil
purchase
pure
purple
purpose
purse
pursue
push
put
puzzle

pyramid
qualification
qualify
quality
quantity
quarrel
quarter
queen
question
questionnaire
queue
quick
quiet
quit
quite
quiz
quotation
quote
rabbit
race
racial
radiation
radio
rail
railway / railroad
rain
rainbow
raincoat
rainfall
rainy
raise
random
range
rank
rapid
rare
rat
rate
rather
rating
raw
ray
razor
reach
react
read
ready
real
realise / realize
reality
really
reason
reasonable
recall
receipt
receive
receiver
recent
reception
recipe

recite
reckon
recognise / recognize
recognition
recommend
record
recorder
recover
recreation
recycle
red
reduce
reduction
refer
referee
reference
reflect
reform
refresh
refrigerator / fridge
refuse
regard
regardless
region
register
registration
regret
regular
regulation
reject
relate
relation
relationship
relative
relax
relay
release
relevant
reliable
relief
relieve
religion
religious
reluctant
rely
remain
remains
remark
remarkable
remember
remind
remote
remove
rent
repair
repeat
replace
reply
report
represent

representative
republic
reputation
request
require
rescue
research
resemble
reservation
reserve
resident
resign
resist
resistant
resolution
resolve
resource
respect
respective
respond
response
responsibility
responsible
rest
restaurant
restore
restrict
restriction
result
resume
retain
retire
return
reveal
revenge
review
revise
revision
revolution
reward
rhyme
rice
rich
rid
riddle
ride
ridiculous
right
rigid
ring
ripe
ripen
rise
risk
river
road
roast
rob
robbery
robot

rock
rocket
role
roll
Roman
romantic
roof
room
root
rope
rose
rot
rotten
rough
round
roundabout
route
routine
row
royal
rubber
rubbish
rude
rugby
ruin
rule
ruler
run
rural
rush
sacred
sacrifice
sad
sadness
safe
safety
sail
sailor
salad
salary
sale
salesman / saleswoman / salesperson
salt
salty
salute
same
sample
sand
sandwich
satellite
satisfaction
satisfactory
satisfy
Saturday
saucer
sausage
save
say
saying
scale

scan
scar
scarce
scare
scarf
scatter
scene
scenery
schedule
scholar
scholarship
school
schoolbag
science
scientific
scientist
scissors
scold
score
scratch
scream
screen
sculpture
sea
seal
search
season
seat
second
secondary
secret
secretary
section
secure
security
see
seed
seek
seem
seize
seldom
select
self
selfish
sell
semester
seminar
send
senior
sense
sensitive
sentence
separate
September
serial
series
serious
servant
serve
service

session
set
setting
settle
settlement
settler
seven
seventeen
seventy
several
severe
sew
sex
shade
shadow
shake
shall
shallow
shame
shape
share
shark
sharp
sharpen
sharpener
shave
she
sheep
sheet
shelf
shell
shelter
shift
shine
ship
shirt
shock
shoe
shoot
shop
shopkeeper
shopping
shore
short
shortage
shortcoming
shortly
shorts
shot
should
shoulder
shout
show
shower
shrink
shut
shuttle
shy
sick
sickness

side
sideways
sigh
sight
sightseeing
sign
signal
signature
significant
silence
silent
silk
silly
silver
similar
simple
simplify
since
sincere
sing
single
sink
sir
sister
sit
site
situation
six
sixteen
sixty
size
skate
skateboard
ski
skilful / skillful
skill
skin
skip
skirt
sky
skyscraper
slave
slavery
sleep
sleepy
sleeve
slice
slide
slight
slim
slip
slow
small
smart
smell
smile
smog
smoke
smoker
smooth

smuggle
snack
snake
sneaker
sneeze
snow
snowy
so
soap
soar
sob
soccer
social
socialism
socialist
society
sock
socket
sofa
soft
software
soil
solar
soldier
solid
solution
solve
some
somebody / someone
somehow
something
sometime
sometimes
somewhat
somewhere
son
song
soon
sorrow
sorry
sort
soul
sound
soup
sour
source
south
southern
souvenir
sow
space
spacious
spare
speak
spear
special
specialist
species
specific
speech

speed
spell
spend
spin
spirit
spiritual
spit
splendid
split
spoken
spokesman / spokeswoman / spokesperson
sponsor
spoon
spoonful
sport
spot
spray
spread
spring
spy
square
squeeze
squirrel
stable
stadium
staff
stage
stain
stair
stamp
stand
standard
star
stare
start
starvation
starve
state
statement
station
statistics
statue
status
stay
steady
steak
steal
steam
steel
steep
step
steward / stewardess
stick
still
stimulate
stocking
stomach
stone
stop

storage
store
storm
story
stove
straight
straightforward
strait
strange
stranger
strategy
straw
strawberry
stream
street
strength
strengthen
stress
stretch
strict
strike
string
strong
structure
struggle
stubborn
student
studio
study
stuff
stupid
style
subject
subjective
submit
subscribe
subsequent
substance
substantial
substitute
subtle
suburb
subway
succeed
success
successful
such
suck
sudden
suffer
sufficient
sugar
suggest
suggestion
suicide
suit
suitable
suitcase
suite
sum

summarise / summarize
summary
summer
summit
sun
sunburn
Sunday
sunlight
sunny
sunshine
super
superb
superficial
superior
supermarket
supervise
supper
supplement
supply
support
suppose
supreme
sure
surf
surface
surgeon
surgery
surname
surplus
surprise
surrender
surround
surroundings
survey
survival
survive
suspect
suspend
suspicion
sustain
swallow
swear
sweat
sweater
sweep
sweet
swell
swift
swim
swing
switch
sword
symbol
sympathetic
sympathy
symphony
symptom
system
table
tablet

tackle
tail
tailor
take
tale
talent
talk
tall
tank
tap
tape
target
task
taste
tax
taxi
taxpayer
tea
teach
teacher
team
teamwork
teapot
tear
tease
technical
technique
technology
teenager
telephone / phone
telescope
television / TV
tell
temper
temperature
temple
temporary
ten
tend
tendency
tennis
tense
tension
tent
term
terminal
terrible
terrific
terrify
territory
terror
test
text
textbook
than
thank
thankful
that
the
theatre / theater

theft
their
theirs
them
theme
themselves
then
theoretical
theory
there
therefore
these
they
thick
thief
thin
thing
think
thinking
third
thirst
thirsty
thirteen
thirty
this
thorough
those
though
thought
thousand

thread
threat
three
thrill
throat
through
throughout
throw
thumb
thunder
Thursday
thus
ticket
tide
tidy
tie
tiger
tight
time
timetable
tin
tiny
tip
tire
tired
tiresome
tissue
title
to
toast

tobacco
today
together
toilet
tolerance
tolerate
tomato
tomb
tomorrow
ton
tone
tongue
tonight
too
tool
tooth
toothache
top
topic
torch
torture
total
touch
tough
tour
tourism
tourist
tournament
towards / toward
towel
tower
town
toy
track
tractor
trade
tradition
traditional
traffic
tragedy
train
training
trait
tram
transfer
transform
translate
translation
transparent
transport
transportation
trap
travel
traveller / traveler
treasure
treat
treatment
treaty
tree
tremble

tremendous
trend
trial
triangle
tribe
trick
trip
triumph
trolleybus
troop
trouble
troublesome
trousers
truck
true
trunk
trust
truth
try
T-shirt
tube
Tuesday
tuition
tune
turkey
turn
tutor
twelfth
twelve
twentieth
twenty
twice
twin
twist
two
type
typewriter
typhoon
typical
typist
tyre / tire
ugly
ultimately
umbrella
unable
uncle
under
undergraduate
underground
underline
understand
undertake
underwear
unfair
uniform
union
unique
unit
unite
universal

universe
university
unless
unlike
until / till
unusual
up
up-to-date
update
upon
upper
upset
upstairs
upwards
urban
urge
urgent
us
use
used
useful
useless
user
usual
usually
vacant
vacation
vacuum
vague
vain
valid
valley
valuable
value
variety
various
vary
vase
vast
vegetable
vehicle
venue
version
vertical
very
vest
via
victim
victory
video
view
village
villager
vinegar
violate
violence
violent
violin
violinist
virtual

virtue
virus
visa
visible
vision
visit
visitor
visual
vital
vivid
vocabulary
voice
volcano
volleyball
volume
voluntary
volunteer
vote
voyage
wage
waist
wait
waiter / waitress
wake
walk
wall
wallet
wander
want
war
ward
warehouse
warm
warmth
warn
wash
washroom
waste
watch
water
watermelon
wave
wax
way
we
weak
weakness
wealth
wealthy
weapon
wear
weather
weave
web
website
wedding
Wednesday
weed
week
weekday

weekend
weekly
weep
weigh
weight
welcome
welfare
well
west
western
wet
whale
what
whatever
wheat
wheel
when
whenever
where
wherever
whether
which
while
whisper
whistle
white
who
whole
whom
whose
why
wide
widespread
wife
wild
wildlife
will
willing
win
wind
window
windy
wine
wing
winter
wipe
wire
wisdom
wise
wish
with
withdraw
within
without
witness
wolf
woman
wonder
wonderful
wood

wool
word
work
worker
workshop
world
worldwide
worm
worry
worse
worship
worst
worth
worthwhile
worthy
would
wound
wrap
wrestle
wrinkle
wrist
write
wrong

X-ray
yard
yawn
year
yell
yellow
yes
yesterday
yet
yield
yoghurt / yogurt
you
young
your
yours
yourself
youth
zero
zip
zone
zoo
zoom

部分国家(或地区)名称及相关信息

国家(或地区)	形容词	人
Afghanistan	Afghan	Afghan
Algeria	Algerian	Algerian
Argentina	Argentinian	Argentinian
Australia	Australian	Australian
Austria	Austrian	Austrian
Belgium	Belgian	Belgian
Brazil	Brazilian	Brazilian
Canada	Canadian	Canadian
China	Chinese	Chinese
Colombia	Colombian	Colombian
Cuba	Cuban	Cuban
Denmark	Danish	Dane
Egypt	Egyptian	Egyptian
England	English	Englishman, Englishwoman; the English
Finland	Finnish	Finn
France	French	Frenchman, Frenchwoman; the French
Germany	German	German
Greece	Greek	Greek
Hungary	Hungarian	Hungarian
India	Indian	Indian
Indonesia	Indonesian	Indonesian
Iran	Iranian	Iranian
Iraq	Iraqi	Iraqi
Ireland	Irish	Irishman, Irishwoman; the Irish

续表

国家(或地区)	形容词	人
Israel	Israeli	Israeli
Italy	Italian	Italian
Japan	Japanese	Japanese
Jordan	Jordanian	Jordanian
Kenya	Kenyan	Kenyan
the Democratic People's Republic of Korea	Korean	Korean
the Republic of Korea	Korean	Korean
Kuwait	Kuwaiti	Kuwaiti
Lebanon	Lebanese	Lebanese
Luxembourg	Luxembourg	Luxembourger
Malaysia	Malaysian	Malaysian
Mexico	Mexican	Mexican
Myanmar	Burmese	Burmese
the Netherlands	Dutch	Dutchman, Dutchwoman; the Dutch
New Zealand	New Zealand	New Zealander
Norway	Norwegian	Norwegian
Pakistan	Pakistani	Pakistani
Panama	Panamanian	Panamanian
the Philippines	Philippine	Filipino
Poland	Polish	Pole
Portugal	Portuguese	Portuguese
Russia	Russian	Russian
Scotland	Scottish	Scot (Scotsman, Scotswoman); the Scots
Singapore	Singaporean	Singaporean
South Africa	South African	South African

续表

国家(或地区)	形容词	人
Spain	Spanish	Spaniard；the Spanish
Sweden	Swedish	Swede；the Swedish
Switzerland	Swiss	Swiss
Thailand	Thai	Thai
Turkey / Türkiye	Turkish	Turk
the United Kingdom / (Great) Britain	British	Briton；the British
the United States (of America) / America	American	American
Vietnam	Vietnamese	Vietnamese
Wales	Welsh	Welshman，Welshwoman；the Welsh

大洲名和大洋名

地理名称	形容词
Africa	African
Antarctica	Antarctic
Asia	Asian
Europe	European
North America	North American
South America	South American
Oceania	Oceanian, Oceanic
the Arctic Ocean	Arctic
the Atlantic Ocean	Atlantic
the Indian Ocean	
the Pacific Ocean	Pacific

民　　法

总　要　求

1. 能够比较准确地理解民法基本概念的内涵与外延，较为系统地掌握民法的基本原理。

2. 能够理解各种基本民事权利，具备在具体社会关系中识别各种民事法律关系的能力，并准确地表述基本民事权利义务的内容。

3. 具备运用所学的民法规范和民法理论分析和解决现实生活中的具体法律问题的能力。

4. 考试内容除大纲规定内容外，每年 6 月 30 日之前经由全国人民代表大会和全国人民代表大会常务委员会颁布的生效法律，也列入考试范围。

考试内容

第一部分　总　　则

一、民法概述

【要求】

理解民法的概念与调整对象。理解我国民法的基本原则。掌握民法的渊源和民法的适用。

（一）民法的概念

（二）民法的调整对象

（三）民法的渊源

1. 制定法

2. 习惯

（四）民法的基本原则

1. 平等原则

2. 自愿原则

3. 公平原则

4. 诚实信用原则

5. 公序良俗原则

6. 绿色原则

（五）民法的适用

1. 民法的适用范围

2. 民法的适用规则

二、民事法律关系

【要求】

理解民事法律关系的概念、特征及要素。掌握民事法律事实的概念、分类及构成。

（一）民事法律关系的概念与特征

1. 民事法律关系的概念

2. 民事法律关系的特征

（二）民事法律关系的要素

1. 民事法律关系的主体

2. 民事法律关系的客体

3. 民事法律关系的内容

民事权利;民事义务。

（三）民事法律事实

1. 民事法律事实的概念

2. 民事法律事实的构成

3. 民事法律事实的分类

三、自然人

【要求】

掌握自然人民事权利能力的概念、开始、胎儿的特殊保护与终止。掌握自然人民事行为能力的概念与种类。掌握自然人住所的认定。掌握监护的概念、监护人的设立、监护人的职责、监护人资格的撤销以及监护的终止。掌握宣告失踪和宣告死亡的概念、条件、程序、效力,以及死亡宣告的撤销。了解个体工商户和农村承包经营户的概念和经营责任承担规则。

（一）自然人的民事权利能力和民事行为能力

1. 自然人的民事权利能力

自然人民事权利能力的概念;自然人民事权利能力的开始与终止;胎儿视为具有民事权利能力的情形。

2. 自然人的民事行为能力

自然人民事行为能力的概念;自然人民事行为能力的种类:完全民事行为能力、限制民事行为能力、无民事行为能力。

3. 自然人的住所

（二）监护

1. 监护的概念

2. 监护人的设立

未成年人监护人的设立;无民事行为能力或者限制民事行为能力的成年人监护人的设立;具有完全民事行为能力的成年人意定监护人的设立。

3. 监护人的职责

4. 监护人资格的撤销

撤销监护人资格的事由;撤销监护人资格的程序;被撤销监护人资格的恢复。

5. 监护的终止

（三）宣告失踪与宣告死亡

1. 宣告失踪

宣告失踪的概念、条件与程序;宣告失踪的效力;失踪宣告的撤销。

2. 宣告死亡

宣告死亡的概念、条件与程序；宣告死亡的效力；死亡宣告的撤销。

（四）个体工商户和农村承包经营户

1. 个体工商户和农村承包经营户的概念

2. 个体工商户和农村承包经营户经营责任承担规则

四、法人

【要求】

了解法人的概念与特征、法人机关的概念。理解我国现行立法对法人的分类。理解法人的民事权利能力、民事行为能力和民事责任能力。理解法人机关构成及法定代表人、法人机关决议（决定）的效力。理解法人的变更、终止与清算。理解法人分支机构的设立与法律地位。掌握法人应具备的条件、法人设立的民事责任。

（一）法人概述

1. 法人的概念与特征

2. 我国现行立法对法人的分类

营利法人；非营利法人；特别法人。

（二）法人的成立

1. 法人应具备的条件

2. 法人资格的取得

3. 法人设立的民事责任

（三）法人的民事能力

1. 法人的民事权利能力

2. 法人的民事行为能力

3. 法人的民事责任能力

（四）法人的机关

1. 法人机关的概念

2. 法人机关构成及法定代表人

3. 法人机关决议（决定）的效力

（五）法人的变更、终止与清算

1. 法人的变更

2. 法人的终止

3. 法人的清算

（六）法人的分支机构

1. 法人分支机构的设立

2. 法人分支机构的法律地位

五、非法人组织

【要求】

了解非法人组织的概念与种类。理解非法人组织的设立、终止和法律地位。

（一）非法人组织的概念与种类

1. 非法人组织的概念

2. 非法人组织的种类

个人独资企业；合伙企业；不具有法人资格的专业服务机构。

（二）非法人组织的设立与终止

1. 非法人组织的设立

2. 非法人组织的终止

（三）非法人组织的法律地位

六、民事权利

【要求】

理解民事权利的概念、特征与分类。理解民事权利的取得、变更、消灭、行使和保护。

（一）民事权利的概念、特征和分类

1. 民事权利的概念

2. 民事权利的特征

3. 民事权利的分类

财产权与人身权；支配权、请求权、形成权与抗辩权；绝对权与相对权；主权利与从权利；专属权与非专属权；既得权与期待权；原权利与救济权。

（二）民事权利的取得、变更和消灭

（三）民事权利的行使

（四）民事权利的保护

1. 公力救济

2. 私力救济

自卫行为；自助行为。

七、民事法律行为

【要求】

理解民事法律行为的概念与特征，了解民事法律行为的分类与形式、意思表示的分类及意义。掌握意思表示的概念、意思与表示的不一致、意思表示的不自由。掌握民事法律行为的成立与生效要件。理解效力待定民事法律行为的概念与特征，掌握欠缺民事行为能力的行为、效力待定民事法律行为的效力确定。理解可撤销民事法律行为的概念，掌握可撤销民事法律行为的种类及撤销权的享有、行使和消灭，民事法律行为被撤销的法律后果。理解无效民事法律行为的概念，掌握无效民事法律行为的种类及民事法律行为被确认无效的法律后果。掌握民事法律行为的附条件与附期限。

（一）民事法律行为概述

1. 民事法律行为的概念与特征

2. 民事法律行为的分类

单方行为、双方行为和多方行为；财产行为与身份行为；要式行为和不要式行为；主行为和从行为。

3. 民事法律行为的形式

口头形式；书面形式；其他形式。

（二）意思表示

1. 意思表示的概念

2. 意思表示的分类及其意义

有相对人的意思表示与无相对人的意思表示；对话的意思表示与非对话的意思表示；明示的意思表示与默示的意思表示；独立的意思表

示与非独立的意思表示。

3. 意思与表示的不一致

单独虚伪表示;通谋虚伪表示;隐藏行为;重大误解。

4. 意思表示的不自由

欺诈;胁迫。

（三）民事法律行为的成立与生效

1. 民事法律行为的成立

2. 民事法律行为的生效

（四）效力待定的民事法律行为

1. 效力待定民事法律行为的概念与特征

2. 效力待定民事法律行为的种类

欠缺民事行为能力的行为;无权代理的行为。

3. 效力待定民事法律行为的效力确定

（五）可撤销的民事法律行为

1. 可撤销的民事法律行为的概念

2. 可撤销的民事法律行为的种类

重大误解的民事法律行为;受欺诈而实施的民事法律行为;受胁迫而实施的民事法律行为;显失公平的民事法律行为。

3. 撤销权的享有、行使和消灭

撤销权的消灭事由。

4. 民事法律行为被撤销的法律后果

（六）无效的民事法律行为

1. 无效民事法律行为的概念

2. 无效民事法律行为的种类

无民事行为能力人实施的民事法律行为;行为人与相对人以虚假的意思表示实施的民事法律行为;违反法律、行政法规的强制性规定的民事法律行为;违背公序良俗的民事法律行为;恶意串通损害他人合法权益的民事法律行为。

3. 民事法律行为无效的法律后果

返还财产;赔偿损失。

（七）民事法律行为的附条件与附期限

1. 附条件的民事法律行为

2. 附期限的民事法律行为

八、代理

【要求】

理解代理的概念、特征、适用范围及代理的类型。了解代理权的概念，理解代理权的发生和代理权的行使。理解无权代理的概念与类型，掌握无权代理的效力及无权代理人的责任。掌握表见代理的概念、构成要件及效力。理解代理权的终止。

（一）代理的概念、特征与适用范围

1. 代理的概念

2. 代理的特征

3. 代理的适用范围

（二）代理的类型

1. 委托代理与法定代理

2. 直接代理与间接代理

3. 本代理与复代理

（三）代理权

1. 代理权的概念

2. 代理权的发生

3. 代理权的行使

代理权行使的原则；滥用代理权的禁止。

（四）无权代理与表见代理

1. 无权代理

无权代理的概念；无权代理的类型；无权代理的效力；无权代理人的责任。

2. 表见代理

表见代理的概念；表见代理的构成要件；表见代理的效力。

（五）代理权的终止

1. 委托代理的终止

2. 法定代理的终止

九、民事责任

【要求】

了解民事责任的概念、特征和分类。理解民事责任的适用。掌握民事责任的承担方式和抗辩事由。

（一）民事责任的概念与特征

1. 民事责任的概念

2. 民事责任的特征

（二）民事责任的分类

1. 违约责任、侵权责任与其他责任

2. 单独责任与共同责任

3. 财产责任与非财产责任

4. 按份责任与连带责任

（三）承担民事责任的方式

1. 停止侵害

2. 排除妨碍

3. 消除危险

4. 返还财产

5. 恢复原状

6. 修理、重作、更换

7. 继续履行

8. 赔偿损失

9. 支付违约金

10. 消除影响、恢复名誉

11. 赔礼道歉

（四）民事责任的抗辩事由

1. 不可抗力

2. 正当防卫

3. 紧急避险

4. 其他法定事由

（五）民事责任的适用

1. 违约责任与侵权责任的竞合

2. 民事责任优先适用原则

十、诉讼时效和期间计算

【要求】

理解诉讼时效的概念、特征和适用范围。理解诉讼时效期间的分类，掌握诉讼时效期间届满的后果。掌握诉讼时效的起算、中止、中断与延长。理解除斥期间的概念与特征。掌握除斥期间与诉讼时效的异同。了解期间的概念与计算方法。

（一）诉讼时效

1. 诉讼时效的概念与特征

2. 诉讼时效的适用范围

3. 诉讼时效期间的分类

4. 诉讼时效期间届满的后果

5. 诉讼时效的起算、中止、中断与延长

6. 除斥期间

除斥期间的概念与特征；除斥期间与诉讼时效的异同。

（二）期间计算

1. 期间的概念

2. 期间的计算方法

第二部分　物　　权

一、物权概述

【要求】

理解物、物权的概念与特征。理解物的分类及其意义、物权的分类、物权法的基本原则。掌握物权变动与物权的保护。

（一）物权的概念与特征

（二）物权的客体

1. 物的概念与特征

2. 物的分类及其意义

动产与不动产；主物与从物；原物与孳息；可分物与不可分物；特定物与种类物；流通物、限制流通物与禁止流通物；有主物与无主物；单一物、合成物与集合物。

（三）物权的分类

1. 所有权和他物权

2. 用益物权和担保物权

3. 动产物权、不动产物权和权利物权

4. 主物权和从物权

5. 意定物权和法定物权

（四）物权法的基本原则

1. 平等保护原则

2. 物权法定原则

3. 物权公示与公信原则

4. 物权客体特定原则

（五）物权的变动

1. 物权变动的概念

2. 基于民事法律行为的物权变动

3. 非基于民事法律行为的物权变动

4. 物权变动的公示方法

动产交付；不动产登记。

（六）物权的保护

1. 确认物权

2. 返还原物

3. 排除妨害或者消除危险

4. 修理、重作、更换或者恢复原状

5. 损害赔偿

二、所有权

【要求】

理解所有权的概念、特征与内容。理解国家所有权、集体所有权与私人所有权。理解业主的建筑物区分所有权的概念、特征，掌握业主的建筑物区分所有权的内容。理解相邻关系的概念与特征，掌握各种相邻关系和处理相邻关系的原则。理解共有的概念与特征，掌握按份共有和共同共有。掌握所有权取得的特别方式。

（一）所有权概述

1. 所有权的概念与特征

2. 所有权的内容

占有；使用；收益；处分。

（二）国家所有权、集体所有权与私人所有权

1. 国家所有权

国家所有权的概念与特征；国家所有权的主体和客体。

2. 集体所有权

集体所有权的概念；集体所有权的主体和客体；集体所有权的行使和保护。

3. 私人所有权

（三）业主的建筑物区分所有权

1. 业主的建筑物区分所有权的概念与特征

2. 业主的建筑物区分所有权的内容

专有部分的所有权；共有部分的共有权；业主的管理权。

（四）相邻关系

1. 相邻关系的概念与特征

2. 各种相邻关系

3. 处理相邻关系的原则

（五）共有

1. 共有的概念与特征

2. 按份共有

按份共有的概念与特征；按份共有产生的根据；按份共有人的内部关系；按份共有人的外部关系；对共有财产的处分或重大修缮；共有财产的分割。

3. 共同共有

共同共有的概念与特征；共同共有与按份共有的区别；共同共有的类型；共同共有人的内部关系；共同共有人的外部关系；对共有财产的处分或重大修缮；共有财产的分割。

（六）所有权取得的特别方式

1. 征收

征收的概念、条件。

2. 善意取得

善意取得的概念、构成要件及法律效果。

3. 拾得遗失物

4. 拾得漂流物、发现埋藏物或隐藏物

5. 添附

附合；混合；加工。

6. 取得孳息

三、用益物权

【要求】

理解用益物权的概念与特征。理解土地承包经营权的概念与特征。掌握土地承包经营权的设立、内容，以及土地经营权的设立与土地经营权人的权利。理解建设用地使用权的概念与特征。掌握建设用地使用权的设立、期限与内容，了解在集体所有的土地上设立的建设用地使用权。理解宅基地使用权的概念、特征及内容。理解居住权的概念与特征，掌握居住权的设立与内容，了解居住权的消灭。理解地役权的概念与特征，掌握地役权的设立与内容，了解地役权的期限与消灭。

（一）用益物权的概念与特征

（二）土地承包经营权

1. 土地承包经营权的概念与特征

2. 土地承包经营权的设立

3. 土地承包经营权的内容

土地承包经营权人的权利；发包人的义务。

4. 土地经营权的设立

5. 土地经营权人的权利

（三）建设用地使用权

1. 建设用地使用权的概念与特征

2. 建设用地使用权的设立与期限

3. 建设用地使用权的内容

建设用地使用权人的权利和义务。

4. 在集体所有的土地上设立的建设用地使用权

（四）宅基地使用权

1. 宅基地使用权的概念与特征

2. 宅基地使用权的内容

宅基地使用权人的权利和义务。

（五）居住权

1. 居住权的概念与特征

2. 居住权的设立

3. 居住权的内容

4. 居住权的消灭

（六）地役权

1. 地役权的概念与特征

2. 地役权的设立

3. 地役权的内容

地役权人的权利和义务；供役地权利人的权利和义务。

4. 地役权的期限

5. 地役权的消灭

四、担保物权

【要求】

理解担保物权的概念、特征与担保物权的分类。掌握担保物权的担保范围，担保物权的竞合与物的担保和人的担保的并存。了解担保物权消灭的情形。理解抵押权的概念与特征。掌握抵押权的设立、抵押权当事人的权利及抵押权的实现，了解动产浮动抵押和最高额抵押。理解质权的概念与特征，掌握动产质权与权利质权。理解留置权的概念与特征，掌握留置权的成立条件，留置权人的权利与义务，留置权的实现与消灭。

（一）担保物权概述

1. 担保物权的概念与特征

2. 担保物权的担保范围

3. 担保物权的分类

法定担保物权与约定担保物权；动产担保物权、不动产担保物权和权利担保物权。

4. 担保物权的竞合与物的担保和人的担保的并存

抵押权与质权的竞合；抵押权与留置权的竞合；质权与留置权的竞合；物的担保与人的担保并存。

5. 担保物权的消灭

（二）抵押权

1. 抵押权的概念与特征

2. 抵押权的设立

抵押合同；抵押登记；可以抵押的财产；不可以抵押的财产。

3. 抵押权的效力

抵押权人的权利；抵押人的权利。

4. 抵押权的实现

抵押权实现的条件；抵押权实现的方式；抵押权实现的顺位；抵押权的实现与诉讼时效。

5. 动产浮动抵押

6. 最高额抵押

（三）质权

1. 质权的概念与特征

2. 动产质权

动产质权的概念；动产质权的设立；动产质权人的权利与义务；动产出质人的权利与义务；动产质权的实现。

3. 权利质权

权利质权的概念；可以出质的权利；权利质权的设立；权利质权当事人的权利与义务；权利质权的实现。

（四）留置权

1. 留置权的概念与特征

2. 留置权的成立条件

3. 留置权的效力

留置权人的权利；留置权人的义务。

4. 留置权的实现

5. 留置权的消灭

五、占有

【要求】

理解占有的概念及分类。掌握占有的效力和保护。

（一）占有概述

1. 占有的概念

2. 占有的分类

有权占有与无权占有；善意占有与恶意占有；直接占有与间接占有；自主占有与他主占有。

（二）占有的效力和保护

1. 占有的效力

2. 占有的保护

占有物返还请求权；排除妨害或者消除危险请求权；损害赔偿请求权。

第三部分　合　　同

一、合同通则

【要求】

理解债的概念、特征、要素及分类。掌握债的发生原因。理解合同的概念与特征，掌握合同的分类，了解债与合同的关系。掌握合同订立的一般程序，理解预约合同的概念。理解合同的内容，了解合同的形式，理解对格式条款的规制，掌握合同成立的时间和地点。理解缔约过失责任的概念，掌握缔约过失责任的构成要件、适用情形及承担方式。理解合同的生效要件及合同效力的特别规则。理解合同履行的一般规则，了解合同履行的特别规则，掌握双务合同履行中的抗辩权。理解情事变更原则的概念，掌握情事变更原则的适用条件及效力。理解合同保全的概念，掌握债权人代位权的概念、成立要件、行使及效力，掌握债权人撤销权的概念、成立要件，理解债权人撤销权的行使及效力。了解合同变更的概念，理解合同变更的要件。掌握合同债权的转让和合同债务的承担，理解合同权利义务的概括移转。理解合同权利义务终止的事由及终止的法律后果，理解抵销的概念，掌握法定抵销和约定抵销的要件，了解抵销的法律后果，理解提存的概念及法律后果，掌握提存的要件，了解免除的概念及法律后果，理解混同的概念及法律后果，掌握合同解除的条件、程序与法律后果。理解违约责任的概念、特征、归责原则，掌握违约责任的构成要件和承担方式，理解违约责任的免责事由。

（一）债与合同概述

1. 债的概述

债的概念、特征；债的要素；债的分类；债的发生原因。

2. 合同概述

合同的概念与特征；合同的分类。

3. 债与合同的关系

(二) 合同的订立

1. 合同订立的程序

要约、承诺;预约合同。

2. 合同的内容和形式

3. 格式条款

4. 合同成立的时间和地点

5. 缔约过失责任

缔约过失责任的概念;缔约过失责任的构成要件;缔约过失责任的适用情形;缔约过失责任的承担方式。

(三) 合同的效力

1. 合同的生效要件

2. 合同效力的特别规则

超越代表权限订立的合同;超越经营范围订立的合同;无效的免责条款。

(四) 合同的履行

1. 合同履行的一般规则

2. 合同履行的特别规则

选择之债的履行规则;连带之债的履行规则。

3. 双务合同履行中的抗辩权

同时履行抗辩权的概念、成立要件及效力;先履行抗辩权的概念、成立要件及效力;不安抗辩权的概念、成立要件、行使及效力。

4. 情事变更原则

情事变更原则的概念;情事变更原则的适用条件;适用情事变更原则的效力。

(五) 合同的保全

1. 合同保全的概念

2. 债权人的代位权

债权人代位权的概念;债权人代位权的成立要件;债权人代位权的行使及效力。

3. 债权人的撤销权

债权人撤销权的概念;债权人撤销权的成立要件;债权人撤销权的行使及效力。

(六) 合同的变更和转让

1. 合同的变更

合同变更的概念;合同变更的要件。

2. 合同债权的转让

债权转让的概念;债权转让合同的有效条件;债权转让的效力。

3.合同债务的承担

债务承担的概念;免责的债务承担的条件及效力;并存的债务承担的条件及效力。

4. 合同权利义务的概括移转

合同权利义务概括移转的概念;合同权利义务概括移转的类型;合同权利义务概括移转的效力。

(七) 合同的权利义务终止

1. 债权债务终止

债权债务终止的概念;后合同义务;债权债务终止的后果。

2. 履行

3. 抵销

抵销的概念;法定抵销的要件;约定抵销的要件;抵销的法律后果。

4. 提存

提存的概念;提存的要件;提存的法律后果。

5. 免除

免除的概念;免除的法律后果。

6. 混同

混同的概念;混同的法律后果。

7. 合同解除

合同解除的条件;合同解除的程序与法律后果。

(八) 违约责任

1. 违约责任的概念与特征

违约责任的概念;违约责任的特征。

2. 违约责任的归责原则

3. 违约责任的构成要件及免责事由

4. 违约责任的承担方式

二、典型合同

【要求】

理解买卖合同、所有权保留买卖合同、赠与合同、借款合同、保证合同、租赁合同、融资租赁合同、保理合同、承揽合同、建设工程合同、运输合同、客运合同、货运合同、技术合同、技术开发合同、技术转让合同、技术许可合同、技术咨询合同、技术服务合同、保管合同、仓储合同、委托合同、物业服务合同、行纪合同、中介合同、合伙合同的概念与特征。了解供用水、电、气、热力合同的概念与当事人的主要义务。掌握买卖合同中出卖人与买受人的主要义务、标的物所有权转移的规则、标的物风险负担的规则和所有权保留买卖合同出卖人的取回权。掌握赠与合同中赠与人的主要义务和赠与合同的撤销。掌握借款合同中贷款人与借款人的主要义务。掌握保证合同的要件、保证的方式、保证担保的范围和保证责任的免除。掌握租赁合同出租人与承租人的主要义务、租赁合同的解除、买卖不破租赁和承租人的优先购买权。掌握融资租赁合同出卖人、出租人与承租人的主要义务。掌握保理合同保理人的权利和义务、以虚构应收账款作为保理合同标的的后果。掌握承揽合同定作人与承揽人的主要义务、承揽合同的解除。掌握建设工程合同中勘察、设计合同当事人的主要义务和施工合同当事人的主要义务。掌握客运合同和货运合同当事人的主要义务。掌握技术合同的效力。掌握技术开发合同、技术转让合同与技术许可合同、技术咨询合同与技术服务合同当事人的主要义务。掌握保管合同中保管人与寄存人的主要义务。掌握仓储合同保管人与存货人的主要义务。掌握委托合同中委托人与受托人的主要义务、委托合同的解除。掌握物业服务合同物业服务人和业主的主要义务。掌握行纪合同委托人与行纪人的主要义务。掌握中介合同委托人与中介人的主要义务。掌握合伙合同中合伙人的权利、义务与责任。

（一）买卖合同

1. 买卖合同的概念与特征

2. 出卖人与买受人的主要义务

3. 标的物所有权转移的规则

4. 标的物风险负担的规则

5. 所有权保留的买卖合同

所有权保留买卖合同的概念;出卖人的取回权。

（二）供用水、电、气、热力合同

1. 供用水、电、气、热力合同的概念

2. 供用水、电、气、热力合同当事人的主要义务

（三）赠与合同

1. 赠与合同的概念与特征

2. 赠与人的主要义务

3. 赠与合同的撤销

（四）借款合同

1. 借款合同的概念与特征

2. 贷款人与借款人的主要义务

（五）保证合同

1. 保证的概念与特征

2. 保证合同的要件

3. 保证的方式

4. 保证担保的范围

5. 保证责任的免除

（六）租赁合同

1. 租赁合同的概念与特征

2. 出租人与承租人的主要义务

3. 租赁合同的解除

4. 租赁合同的特别效力

买卖不破租赁;承租人的优先购买权。

（七）融资租赁合同

1. 融资租赁合同的概念与特征

2. 出卖人、出租人与承租人的主要义务

（八）保理合同

1. 保理合同的概念与特征

2. 保理人的权利和义务

3. 以虚构应收账款作为保理合同标的的后果

（九）承揽合同

1. 承揽合同的概念与特征

2. 定作人与承揽人的主要义务

3. 承揽合同的解除

（十）建设工程合同

1. 建设工程合同的概念与特征

2. 勘察、设计合同当事人的主要义务

3. 施工合同当事人的主要义务

（十一）运输合同

1. 运输合同的概念与特征

2. 客运合同

客运合同的概念与特征；客运合同当事人的主要义务。

3. 货运合同

货运合同的概念与特征；货运合同当事人的主要义务。

（十二）技术合同

1. 技术合同的概念与特征

2. 技术合同的效力

3. 技术开发合同

技术开发合同的概念与特征；技术开发合同当事人的主要义务。

4. 技术转让合同与技术许可合同

技术转让合同与技术许可合同的概念与特征；技术转让合同与技术许可合同当事人的主要义务。

5. 技术咨询合同与技术服务合同

技术咨询合同与技术服务合同的概念与特征；技术咨询合同与技

术服务合同当事人的主要义务。

（十三）保管合同

1. 保管合同的概念与特征

2. 保管人与寄存人的主要义务

（十四）仓储合同

1. 仓储合同的概念与特征

2. 保管人与存货人的主要义务

（十五）委托合同

1. 委托合同的概念与特征

2. 委托人与受托人的主要义务

3. 委托合同的解除

（十六）物业服务合同

1. 物业服务合同的概念与特征

2. 物业服务人和业主的主要义务

（十七）行纪合同

1. 行纪合同的概念与特征

2. 委托人与行纪人的主要义务

（十八）中介合同

1. 中介合同的概念与特征

2. 委托人与中介人的主要义务

（十九）合伙合同

1. 合伙合同的概念与特征

2. 合伙人的权利、义务与责任

三、准合同

【要求】

掌握无因管理的概念、无因管理之债的构成要件和效力。掌握不当得利的概念、不当得利之债的构成要件和效力。理解不当得利之债的类型。

（一）无因管理

1. 无因管理的概念
2. 无因管理之债的构成要件
3. 无因管理之债的效力
（二）不当得利
1. 不当得利的概念
2. 不当得利之债的构成要件
3. 不当得利之债的类型
4. 不当得利之债的效力

第四部分　人　格　权

一、人格权概述

【要求】

理解人格权的概念、分类与特征。

（一）人格权的概念

（二）人格权的分类

一般人格权；具体人格权。

（三）人格权的特征

二、生命权、身体权和健康权

【要求】

理解生命权、身体权、健康权的概念、特征与内容。

（一）生命权

1. 生命权的概念与特征
2. 生命权的内容

（二）身体权

1. 身体权的概念与特征
2. 身体权的内容

（三）健康权

1. 健康权的概念与特征

2. 健康权的内容

三、姓名权与名称权

【要求】

理解姓名权、名称权的概念、特征与内容。

（一）姓名权

1. 姓名权的概念与特征

2. 姓名权的内容

（二）名称权

1. 名称权的概念与特征

2. 名称权的内容

四、肖像权

【要求】

理解肖像权的概念、特征与内容。

（一）肖像权的概念与特征

1. 肖像权的概念

2. 肖像权的特征

（二）肖像权的内容

五、名誉权和荣誉权

【要求】

理解名誉权、荣誉权的概念、特征与内容。

（一）名誉权

1. 名誉权的概念与特征

2. 名誉权的内容

（二）荣誉权

1. 荣誉权的概念与特征

2. 荣誉权的内容

六、隐私权和个人信息

【要求】

理解隐私权的概念、特征、范围与内容。了解个人信息的概念与范围,理解个人信息的保护。

(一) 隐私权

1. 隐私权的概念、特征与范围

2. 隐私权的内容

(二) 个人信息保护

1. 个人信息的概念与范围

2. 个人信息的保护

第五部分　婚姻家庭

一、亲属

【要求】

理解亲属的概念、特征与种类。掌握亲系的概念、分类,了解亲等的概念,掌握我国采用的世代计算法。理解近亲属的范围和家庭成员认定。

(一) 亲属的概念与特征

(二) 亲属的种类

1. 配偶

2. 血亲

血亲的概念;血亲的类型。

3. 姻亲

(三) 亲系与亲等

1. 亲系的概念

2. 亲系的分类

直系血亲和旁系血亲;直系姻亲和旁系姻亲。

3. 亲等

亲等的概念;我国采用的世代计算法。

(四) 近亲属与家庭成员

1. 近亲属的范围

2. 家庭成员的认定

二、结婚

【要求】

掌握结婚的实质条件与形式条件。理解事实婚姻制度。掌握无效婚姻与可撤销婚姻。

(一) 结婚条件

1. 结婚的实质条件

结婚的必备条件;结婚的禁止条件。

2. 结婚的形式条件

(二) 事实婚姻

1. 事实婚姻的概念

2. 补办结婚登记的效力

3. 未补办结婚登记的效力

(三) 无效婚姻

1. 无效婚姻的概念

2. 婚姻无效的情形

3. 无效婚姻的宣告程序

4. 无效婚姻的法律后果

人身关系方面的后果;财产关系方面的后果;父母子女方面的后果;损害赔偿责任。

(四) 可撤销婚姻

1. 可撤销婚姻的概念

2. 婚姻可撤销的情形

3. 撤销婚姻的程序

4. 婚姻被撤销的法律后果

三、家庭关系

【要求】

理解夫妻人身关系。掌握夫妻财产关系。掌握父母子女关系。理解祖孙关系和兄弟姐妹关系。

（一）夫妻关系

1. 夫妻人身关系

夫妻的姓名权；夫妻的人身自由权；夫妻对抚育未成年子女有平等的权利和义务；夫妻的相互忠实义务。

2. 夫妻财产关系

夫妻法定财产制的内容；夫妻约定财产制的内容；夫妻有相互扶养的义务；夫妻有相互继承权；夫妻有日常家事代理权。

（二）父母子女关系

1. 父母对子女有抚养的义务

2. 父母有教育、保护未成年子女的权利和义务

3. 子女对父母有赡养扶助的义务

4. 子女有不得干涉父母婚姻的义务

5. 父母和子女有相互继承遗产的权利

6. 父、母或成年子女对亲子关系有请求确认或否认的权利

（三）其他近亲属关系

1. 祖孙关系

祖孙之间的抚养义务和赡养义务；祖孙之间承担抚养义务和赡养义务的条件。

2. 兄弟姐妹关系

兄弟姐妹之间的扶养义务；兄弟姐妹之间承担扶养义务的条件。

四、离婚

【要求】

理解离婚的概念与特征。理解登记离婚的概念、条件和程序。了解诉讼离婚的概念，理解诉讼离婚的调解制度，理解诉讼离婚的特殊保

护规定,掌握判决离婚的法定理由、离婚的法律后果和离婚时的救济。

（一）离婚的概念与特征

（二）登记离婚

1. 登记离婚的概念

2. 登记离婚的条件

3. 登记离婚的程序

（三）诉讼离婚

1. 诉讼离婚的概念

2. 诉讼离婚的调解制度

诉讼外调解;诉讼中调解。

3. 诉讼离婚的特殊保护规定

对现役军人的特殊保护;对女方的特殊保护。

4. 判决离婚的法定理由

（四）离婚的法律后果

1. 在身份关系方面的后果

2. 在财产关系方面的后果

3. 在父母子女关系方面的后果

（五）离婚时的救济

1. 离婚时的经济补偿

2. 离婚时的经济帮助

3. 离婚损害赔偿

五、收养

【要求】

理解收养的概念与特征。掌握收养关系成立的实质条件和形式条件。理解收养的效力。理解收养关系解除的法定情形、程序及法律后果。

（一）收养的概念与特征

（二）收养关系的成立

1. 收养关系成立的实质条件

一般收养关系成立的条件;特殊收养关系成立的条件。

2. 收养关系成立的形式条件

(三) 收养的效力

1. 收养的拟制效力

2. 收养的解消效力

3. 收养行为的无效

(四) 收养关系的解除

1. 收养关系解除的法定情形

2. 收养关系解除的程序

3. 收养关系解除的法律后果

第六部分 继 承

一、继承概述

【要求】

理解继承的概念与特征。掌握继承的开始与继承的接受。理解继承权的概念与特征。掌握继承权的放弃与继承权的丧失。理解遗产的概念与范围。

(一) 继承的概念与特征

(二) 继承的开始与继承的接受

(三) 继承权的概念与特征

(四) 继承权的放弃

1. 继承权放弃的概念

2. 放弃继承权的时间、方式

3. 继承权放弃的效力

(五) 继承权的丧失

1. 继承权丧失的概念

2. 继承权丧失的法定事由

3. 继承权丧失的效力

（六）遗产

1. 遗产的概念

2. 遗产的范围

二、法定继承

【要求】

理解法定继承的概念与特征。掌握法定继承人的范围与继承顺序。掌握代位继承。理解遗产中适用法定继承的情形。理解法定继承的遗产分配原则及非继承人对遗产的取得。

（一）法定继承的概念与特征

（二）法定继承人的范围与继承顺序

（三）代位继承

（四）遗产中适用法定继承的情形

（五）法定继承的遗产分配

1. 法定继承的遗产分配原则

2. 非继承人对遗产的取得

三、遗嘱继承和遗赠

【要求】

理解遗嘱继承的概念与特征，掌握遗嘱继承的适用条件。理解遗嘱的概念与特征。掌握遗嘱的形式和遗嘱的有效条件。理解遗嘱的无效、变更与撤回。理解遗赠的概念与特征，掌握遗赠与遗嘱继承的区别。

（一）遗嘱继承的概念与特征

（二）遗嘱继承的适用条件

（三）遗嘱的概念与特征

（四）遗嘱的形式

自书遗嘱；代书遗嘱；打印遗嘱；录音录像遗嘱；口头遗嘱；公证遗嘱。

（五）遗嘱的有效条件

1. 遗嘱人须有遗嘱能力

2. 遗嘱所处分的财产须为遗嘱人的个人财产

3. 遗嘱须是遗嘱人的真实意思表示

4. 遗嘱内容须合法

5. 遗嘱形式须合法

（六）遗嘱的无效

1. 遗嘱无效的概念

2. 遗嘱无效的情形

（七）遗嘱的变更与撤回

（八）遗赠

1. 遗赠的概念与特征

2. 遗赠与遗嘱继承的区别

四、遗产的处理

【要求】

理解遗产管理人的产生、职责和责任。理解转继承和遗产的析产。掌握遗赠扶养协议的概念、特征及效力。理解遗产债务的清偿与遗产的分割。了解无人承受遗产的处理。

（一）遗产管理人

1. 遗产管理人的产生

2. 遗产管理人的职责

3. 遗产管理人的责任

（二）转继承

（三）遗产的析产

（四）遗赠扶养协议

1. 遗赠扶养协议的概念与特征

2. 遗赠扶养协议的效力

（五）遗产债务的清偿

1. 遗产债务的概念

2. 遗产债务的清偿原则

限定继承原则；保留必留份原则；清偿债务优先于执行遗赠原则；继承人之间的责任。

3. 继承人对遗产债务的清偿顺序

（六）遗产的分割

1. 遗产分割的概念

2. 遗产分割的原则

遗产分割自由原则；保留胎儿继承份额原则；互谅互让、协商分割原则；物尽其用原则。

（七）无人承受遗产的处理

第七部分　侵权责任

一、侵权责任概述

【要求】

理解侵权责任的概念、特征和侵权责任归责原则的概念。理解过错责任原则的概念与特征。掌握过错责任原则的适用范围。理解无过错责任原则的概念与特征。掌握无过错责任原则的适用范围。

（一）侵权责任的概念与特征

（二）侵权责任的归责原则

1. 侵权责任归责原则的概念

2. 过错责任原则

过错责任原则的概念与特征；过错责任原则的适用范围。

3. 无过错责任原则

无过错责任原则的概念与特征；无过错责任原则的适用范围。

二、一般侵权责任的构成要件

【要求】

掌握一般侵权责任的构成要件。

（一）加害行为

（二）损害事实

（三）因果关系

（四）主观过错

三、损害赔偿

【要求】

理解人身损害赔偿、财产损失赔偿、精神损害赔偿、惩罚性赔偿和法定的损失分担规则的概念。掌握人身损害赔偿的赔偿范围、财产损失赔偿数额的确定、精神损害赔偿的适用范围、惩罚性赔偿的适用范围和法定的损失分担规则的适用。

（一）人身损害赔偿

1. 人身损害赔偿的概念

2. 人身损害赔偿的赔偿范围

（二）财产损失赔偿

1. 财产损失赔偿的概念

2. 财产损失赔偿数额的确定

（三）精神损害赔偿

1. 精神损害赔偿的概念

2. 精神损害赔偿的适用范围

（四）惩罚性赔偿

1. 惩罚性赔偿的概念

2. 惩罚性赔偿的适用范围

（五）法定的损失分担规则

1. 法定的损失分担规则的概念

2. 法定的损失分担规则的适用

四、数人侵权行为及其责任

【要求】

理解数人侵权行为、共同侵权行为、教唆行为、帮助行为、共同危险行为和无意思联络的数人侵权行为的概念。掌握共同侵权行为的构成要件、共同侵权行为的责任、教唆行为和帮助行为的责任、共同危险行为的构成要件、共同危险行为的责任、无意思联络的数人侵权行为的责任。

（一）数人侵权行为的概念

（二）共同侵权行为及其责任

1. 共同侵权行为的概念

2. 共同侵权行为的构成要件

行为人为二人以上；行为的关联性；共同的过错；结果的单一性。

3. 共同侵权行为的责任

（三）教唆行为、帮助行为及其责任

1. 教唆行为、帮助行为的概念

2. 教唆行为、帮助行为的责任

（四）共同危险行为及其责任

1. 共同危险行为的概念

2. 共同危险行为的构成要件

3. 共同危险行为的责任

（五）无意思联络的数人侵权行为及其责任

1. 无意思联络的数人侵权行为的概念

2. 无意思联络的数人侵权行为的责任

五、不承担责任和减轻责任的情形

【要求】

掌握不承担责任和减轻责任的各种情形及其认定。

（一）受害人故意

（二）第三人原因

（三）自甘风险

（四）自助

（五）被侵权人过错

（六）其他法定免责事由

六、特殊责任主体的侵权责任

【要求】

理解监护人责任、违反安全保障义务侵权责任、教育机构侵权责任的概念。掌握监护人责任的承担、用人单位工作人员职务侵权行为及责任、个人劳务关系中的侵权行为及责任、网络用户的侵权责任、网络服务提供者的侵权责任、违反安全保障义务侵权责任的构成要件及责任承担、教育机构侵权责任的构成要件及责任承担。了解完全民事行为能力人暂时丧失意识的侵权责任。

（一）监护人责任

1. 监护人责任的概念

2. 监护人责任的承担

（二）完全民事行为能力人暂时丧失意识的侵权责任

1. 完全民事行为能力人暂时丧失意识侵权责任的概念

2. 完全民事行为能力人暂时丧失意识侵权责任的承担

（三）用人者责任

1. 用人单位工作人员职务侵权行为及责任

2. 个人劳务关系中的侵权行为及责任

（四）网络侵权责任

1. 网络用户的侵权责任

2. 网络服务提供者的侵权责任

（五）违反安全保障义务的侵权责任

1. 违反安全保障义务侵权责任的概念

2. 违反安全保障义务侵权责任的构成要件

3. 违反安全保障义务侵权责任的承担

（六）教育机构的侵权责任

1. 教育机构侵权责任的概念

2. 教育机构侵权责任的构成要件

3. 教育机构侵权责任的承担

七、产品责任

【要求】

理解产品责任的概念。掌握产品责任的归责原则、构成要件、责任主体及责任承担。

（一）产品责任的概念

（二）产品责任的归责原则和构成要件

（三）产品责任的责任主体

（四）产品责任的承担

八、机动车交通事故责任

【要求】

理解机动车交通事故责任的概念。掌握机动车交通事故责任的归责原则、构成要件、类型及责任承担。

（一）机动车交通事故责任的概念

（二）机动车交通事故责任的归责原则与构成要件

（三）机动车交通事故责任的类型及责任承担

九、医疗损害责任

【要求】

理解医疗损害责任和医疗产品责任的概念。掌握医疗损害责任的构成要件及责任承担。掌握医疗产品责任的承担。

（一）医疗损害责任的概念

（二）医疗损害责任的构成要件

（三）医疗损害责任的承担

（四）医疗产品责任

1. 医疗产品责任的概念

2. 医疗产品责任的承担

十、环境污染和生态破坏责任

【要求】

理解环境污染和生态破坏责任的概念。掌握环境污染和生态破坏责任的构成要件及责任承担。

（一）环境污染和生态破坏责任的概念

（二）环境污染和生态破坏责任的构成要件

（三）环境污染和生态破坏责任的承担

十一、高度危险责任

【要求】

理解高度危险责任的概念与特征。掌握高度危险责任的构成要件和责任承担。

（一）高度危险责任的概念与特征

（二）高度危险责任的构成要件

（三）高度危险责任的承担

十二、饲养动物损害责任

【要求】

理解饲养动物损害责任的概念与特征。掌握饲养动物损害责任的构成要件和责任承担。

（一）饲养动物损害责任的概念与特征

（二）饲养动物损害责任的构成要件

（三）饲养动物损害责任的承担

十三、建筑物和物件损害责任

【要求】

理解建筑物和物件损害责任的概念。掌握建筑物、构筑物或者其他设施致人损害的责任。掌握建筑物抛掷物、坠落物致人损害的责任与补偿。掌握物件致人损害的责任。

（一）建筑物和物件损害责任的概念

（二）建筑物、构筑物或者其他设施致人损害的责任

（三）建筑物抛掷物、坠落物致人损害的责任与补偿

（四）物件致人损害的责任

考试形式及试卷结构

试卷总分：150 分

考试时间：150 分钟

考试方式：闭卷，笔试

试卷内容比例：

总则部分	约 20%
物权部分	约 20%
合同部分	约 25%
人格权部分 婚姻家庭部分 继承部分	约 20%
侵权责任部分	约 15%

试卷题型比例：

选择题	约 46%
简答题	约 20%
论述题	约 14%
案例分析题	约 20%

样　　题

一、选择题：1～35 小题，每小题 2 分，共 70 分。在每小题给出的四个选项中，只有一项是最符合题目要求的。

1. 下列情形中，可以形成民事法律关系的是

A. 甲到寺庙求签拜佛　　B. 乙在家中饮茶会友

C. 丙从网店购买海鲜 D. 丁与同学相约逛街

2. 甲雇钟点工乙打扫卫生,乙向甲主张劳务费的权利属于

A. 支配权 B. 请求权

C. 形成权 D. 抗辩权

3. 甲、乙婚后育有一子,尚未成年。现甲因突发疾病而丧失民事行为能力。甲的监护人应是

A. 乙 B. 甲之父

C. 甲之母 D. 甲之子

4. 下列选项中,属于营利法人的是

A. 基金会 B. 教育局

C. 民政局 D. 股份有限公司

5. 代理人超越代理权所签订合同的效力是

A. 无效 B. 可撤销

C. 有效 D. 效力待定

6. 甲对乙说:“如果你考试过关,就送你一个手机。”乙欣然同意。该约定中的“考试过关”属于

A. 解除条件 B. 延缓条件

C. 延缓期限 D. 解除期限

7. 甲向乙购买一批建材,合同签订后得知自己对建材的规格存在重大误解。甲请求撤销该合同的期限为

A. 90 日 B. 1 年

C. 2 年 D. 4 年

8. 甲、乙签订买卖合同,约定:“本合同不适用诉讼时效规定。”该条款的效力为

A. 有效 B. 无效

C. 可撤销 D. 效力待定

9. 甲被乙踢伤,其向乙请求赔偿的诉讼时效期间为

A. 1 年 B. 2 年

C. 3 年 D. 4 年

10. 下列选项中,不属于民法上的物的是

A. 田里的水稻 B. 池中的鱼儿

C. 地下的管线 D. 正午的太阳

11. 下列选项中，属于物权的是

A. 租赁权 B. 居住权

C. 著作权 D. 名誉权

12. 村民甲于3月1日获批宅基地，4月1日开始建房，9月1日完工，11月1日办理房屋所有权登记。甲取得房屋所有权的时间是

A. 3月1日 B. 4月1日

C. 9月1日 D. 11月1日

13. 张某误将邻居存放门口的一块木料用于建造房屋，现木料已无法拆除。张某依法取得该木料所有权的方式是

A. 善意取得 B. 附合

C. 加工 D. 混合

14. 下列选项中，属于用益物权的是

A. 所有权 B. 地役权

C. 抵押权 D. 留置权

15. 村民甲承包本村耕地，其取得土地承包经营权的时间为

A. 承包合同成立时 B. 承包合同生效时

C. 承包经营权登记时 D. 承包经营权颁证时

16. 担保物权存续期间，担保物被分割的，担保物权人仍有权就担保物的全部行使权利，这一特性称为担保物权的

A. 从属性 B. 物上代位性

C. 不可分性 D. 独立性

17. 甲向乙借款10万元，以价值15万元的房屋设立抵押权并办理了登记。后房屋因失火灭失，甲获得保险赔偿金5万元。乙有权主张优先受偿的数额为

A. 5万元 B. 10万元

C. 15万元 D. 20万元

18. 下列依法可以转让的权利中，不能设定权利质押的是

A. 宅基地使用权 B. 股权

C. 专利权　　D. 基金份额

19. 甲将衣物送洗衣店清洗,事后未付洗衣费,洗衣店依法将衣物扣留。洗衣店行使的权利是

A. 留置权　　B. 动产质权

C. 抵押权　　D. 权利质权

20. 甲将一幅字画交付给乙设定质押担保。乙对该字画的占有属于

A. 自主占有　　B. 间接占有

C. 善意占有　　D. 有权占有

21. 甲对乙说:“你借的钱不用还了。”乙表示同意。甲、乙之间债务消灭的原因是

A. 混同　　B. 免除

C. 抵销　　D. 清偿

22. 甲与乙签订供货合同,未约定先后履行顺序。在供货前,甲请求乙先付款,乙表示一手交钱一手交货。乙的主张属于行使

A. 同时履行抗辩权　　B. 先诉抗辩权

C. 先履行抗辩权　　D. 不安抗辩权

23. 下列选项中,属于要约的是

A. 投标　　B. 发布拍卖公告

C. 寄送价目表　　D. 刊登招股说明书

24. 甲承租乙的房屋并订立合同,该合同为

A. 委托合同　　B. 买卖合同

C. 租赁合同　　D. 中介合同

25. 下列选项中,构成不当得利的是

A. 诉讼时效期满后的清偿　　B. 房屋购买后价格上涨

C. 某公司清偿未到期债务　　D. 售货员多找了的零钱

26. 甲未到法定婚龄而与乙结婚,其婚姻效力为

A. 无效　　B. 可撤销

C. 有效　　D. 效力待定

27. 夫妻在婚姻关系存续期间取得的下列财产,为夫妻一方个人财产的是

A. 工资　　　　　　　　　　B. 劳务报酬

C. 奖金　　　　　　　　　　D. 人身损害赔偿金

28. 张某勇斗歹徒，不幸牺牲。下列财产中，属于张某遗产的是

A. 租的房屋　　　　　　　　B. 抚恤金

C. 借的书籍　　　　　　　　D. 所持股票

29. 下列人员中，可以作为遗嘱见证人的是

A. 遗嘱人的配偶　　　　　　B. 遗嘱人的儿媳

C. 遗嘱人的同事　　　　　　D. 遗嘱人的女婿

30. 受遗赠人得知受遗赠后逾 60 日既不表示接受，也不表示放弃的，视为

A. 放弃受遗赠　　　　　　　B. 接受遗赠

C. 转继承　　　　　　　　　D. 代位继承

31. 村民刘某与同村孤寡老人王某签订一份遗赠扶养协议，该协议的成立时间是

A. 双方所在村委会同意时　　B. 双方意思表示一致时

C. 王某死亡时　　　　　　　D. 王某遗产分割时

32. 甲将一辆拼装汽车出售给乙，乙违章驾驶该车将丙撞伤。丙的损害应由

A. 甲独自承担赔偿责任　　　B. 乙独自承担赔偿责任

C. 甲和乙承担连带赔偿责任　D. 甲和乙承担按份赔偿责任

33. 甲用木棍捅了蜂农乙家的蜂箱，蜜蜂倾巢而出，将路人丙蜇伤。对此，丙

A. 只能向甲请求赔偿　　　　B. 只能向乙请求赔偿

C. 自行承担损害后果　　　　D. 有权请求甲或乙承担赔偿责任

34. 周某在甲医院输入乙血库提供的血液制品而感染病毒。周某的损害

A. 只能向甲医院请求赔偿

B. 只能向乙血库请求赔偿

C. 有权请求甲医院或乙血库承担赔偿责任

D. 由其自行承担

35. 甲超市购买乙公司生产的鲜牛肉。因丙公司的运输车不符合要

求,鲜牛肉受到污染。丁食用了从甲超市购买的鲜牛肉导致腹泻。丁的损害

A. 只能向甲超市请求赔偿

B. 只能向乙公司请求赔偿

C. 有权向丙公司请求赔偿

D. 有权向甲超市或乙公司请求赔偿

二、简答题:36～38 小题,每小题 10 分,共 30 分。

36. 简答自然人民事行为能力的种类。

37. 简答所有权的内容。

38. 简答人格权的特征。

三、论述题:39 小题,20 分。

39. 论述无因管理的概念及构成要件。

四、案例分析题:40～41 小题,每小题 15 分,共 30 分。

40.【案例】刘某拿着自己的一张艺术照到甲装裱店进行装裱,支付装裱费 2000 元。后刘某发现,自己的艺术照被甲装裱店用于其网站的商业宣传。为此引起纠纷。

请回答:

(1) 刘某与甲装裱店之间存在何种合同关系?为什么?

(2) 甲装裱店的商业宣传行为侵犯了刘某的何种人格权?为什么?

41.【案例】两名小学生李某和王某放学后在路边玩耍,两人相互扔石子时,其中一个石子砸伤路人赵某。李某和王某赶紧联系家长将赵某送医,为此花去治疗费若干。经查,无法确定是谁扔的石子砸中赵某,且李某和王某均无个人财产。

请回答:

(1) 李某和王某扔石子的行为是否构成共同危险行为?为什么?

(2) 赵某是否有权请求李某和王某双方的家长承担连带责任?为什么?

参考答案

一、选择题

1. C	2. B	3. A	4. D	5. D
6. B	7. A	8. B	9. C	10. D
11. B	12. C	13. B	14. B	15. B
16. C	17. A	18. A	19. A	20. D
21. B	22. A	23. A	24. C	25. D
26. A	27. D	28. D	29. C	30. A
31. B	32. C	33. D	34. C	35. D

二、简答题

36. **答案要点：**

完全民事行为能力;限制民事行为能力;无民事行为能力。

37. **答案要点：**

占有;使用;收益;处分。

38. **答案要点：**

是民事主体依法所固有的基本权利;是民事主体专有的民事权利;以民事主体的人格利益为客体。

三、论述题

39. **答案要点：**

无因管理是指没有法定或约定的义务,为避免他人利益受损失而对他人进行事务的管理或服务的行为。其构成要件为:管理他人事务;为他人利益而管理;没有法定或约定义务。

四、案例分析题

40. **答案要点：**

(1) 承揽合同。承揽人按照定作人的要求完成工作,交付工作成果,定作人支付报酬的合同是承揽合同。

(2) 肖像权。未经他人允许使用他人肖像的行为构成侵害肖像权。

41. **答案要点:**

(1) 构成。两人的行为危及他人人身和财产安全且造成损害后果,无法确定实际侵害人,符合共同危险行为的构成要件。

(2) 有权。被监护人实施共同危险行为致人损害,且无个人财产,应由监护人承担连带责任。

教育理论

总　要　求

教育学部分

1. 理解和掌握教育学的基础知识、基本理论，把握当前教育理论与实践中的热点问题。

2. 识记教育学的基本概念，对教育学体系中的基础知识和基本理论，如教育学的研究对象、教育学的发展历程、教育的本质、教育功能、教育基本规律、教育目的、教育制度、教师和学生、教学理论和实践、德育理论和实践、班主任工作、课外校外教育等有比较全面准确的认识和理解。

3. 能综合运用教育学的基础知识和基本理论分析教育的现实问题，初步具有分析和解决教育和教学实践问题的能力。

4. 在考试之日起前 6 个月，由全国人民代表大会和国务院颁布或修订的法律、法规都将列入相应课程的考试范围。凡大纲、教材内容与现行法律、法规不符的，应以现行法律法规为准。命题时也会体现关于我国经济建设和科技文化发展的重大方针政策的变化。

心理学部分

1. 识记心理学的基本概念、心理现象的分类及其特征。

2. 理解并掌握心理学研究对象、方法和心理学基本理论，感觉和知觉、注意、记忆、思维和想象、情绪与意志、需要与动机、技能、能力、人格、社会态度与行为、心理健康和心理咨询等心理活动的原理和规律。

3. 运用心理学的概念、原理、理论与方法，对教育教学工作及日常生活中的心理学问题进行分析、辨别、解释和说明。

4. 能够综合运用心理学理论与知识，分析当前学校教育教学及社会生活中的心理学问题，并提出解决问题的心理学依据与策略，具备分析与处理教育实践问题的能力。

考 试 内 容

教育学部分

一、绪论

【要求】

1. 掌握教育学的研究对象和任务。

2. 理解教育学发展的几个主要阶段以及各阶段的概况，识记各阶段的主要教育家及其代表作、主要教育观点。

3. 理解当代教育学的发展趋势、新的教育理论和思想以及学习教育学对教育教学工作的意义。

（一）教育学的研究对象和任务

1. 教育学的研究对象

教育学是研究教育现象和教育问题，揭示教育规律的一门学科。教育现象包括教育社会现象和教育认识现象；教育现象被认识和研究，便成为教育问题；教育规律是教育内部诸因素之间、教育与外部诸因素之间内在的本质的必然的联系，也可称之为教育内部规律和教育外部规律。

2. 教育学的研究任务

阐明教育的基础知识和基本理论，揭示教育教学的基本规律，给教育理论和实践工作者以理论和方法的指导，全面提高教育教学质量，为新的历史时期培养合格的人才服务。

3. 教育学与教育方针政策、教育实践经验的关系

(1) 教育学不等于教育方针政策。

(2) 教育学不等于教育实践经验。

4. 教育学与教育科学

教育科学已形成一个具有多个分支学科的庞大的科学体系,教育学是庞大教育科学体系中的基础学科。

(二) 教育学的发展概况

1. 教育学的萌芽阶段

我国战国末年出现的世界上第一部教育文献《学记》、老子的《老子》、庄子的《庄子》、孔子的《论语》、孟子的《孟子》、无名氏的《大学》、韩愈的《师说》、朱熹的《四书集注》、王守仁的《传习录》等,西方柏拉图的《理想国》、亚里士多德的《政治学》、昆体良的《论演说家的教育》(又译为《雄辩术原理》)等都是反映这个阶段的相关文献。

2. 独立形态教育学的产生

英国哲学家培根作为近代实验科学的鼻祖,提出归纳法,为教育学的发展奠定了方法论基础,首次把教育学作为一门独立的学科提了出来;德国哲学家康德首次将教育学作为一门课程在大学讲授。

捷克教育家夸美纽斯 1632 年出版的《大教学论》,被看作近代第一部系统论述教育问题的教育学专著。其后,陆续出现了一系列对后世有影响的教育家及教育代表作:[英]洛克的《教育漫话》、[法]卢梭的《爱弥儿》、[瑞]裴斯泰洛齐的《林哈德和葛笃德》、[德]赫尔巴特的《普通教育学》、[德]福禄贝尔的《人的教育》、[英]斯宾塞的《教育论》、[俄]乌申斯基的《人是教育的对象》、[美]杜威的《民本主义与教育》。夸美纽斯、赫尔巴特、杜威主要的教育理论观点。

我国的王国维先生于 1901 年翻译了日本立花铣三郎编著的《教育学》,这是引进中国的第一本全文翻译的《教育学》。王国维于 1905 年编著了一本《教育学》,这是国人编著的第一本《教育学》。

3. 马克思主义教育学的建立

苏联教育家克鲁普斯卡娅的《国民教育与民主制度》、加里宁的《论共产主义教育》、马卡连柯的《论共产主义教育》和《教育诗》、凯洛夫的

《教育学》及主要理论观点。

20 世纪初随着马克思主义传入中国，并与中国共产党领导的中央苏区和解放区教育实践相结合，产生了新民主主义教育思想。代表人物有陈独秀、李大钊、毛泽东、恽代英、杨贤江等。其中杨贤江的《新教育大纲》(1930 年)是我国最早以马克思主义为指导系统地论述教育问题的著作。此外还有孟宪承的《教育概论》、舒新城的《教育通论》等。

4. 现代教育学发展中逐渐形成的理论派别

(1) 实验教育学　德国教育家梅伊曼的《实验教育学纲要》和拉伊的《实验教育学》。实验教育学的主要观点。

(2) 文化教育学(又称精神科学教育学)　德国教育家狄尔泰的《关于普遍妥当的教育学的可能》、斯普朗格的《教育与文化》、利特的《职业陶冶、专业教育、人的陶冶》。文化教育学的主要观点。

(3) 实用主义教育学　美国教育家杜威的《民本主义与教育》、克伯屈的《设计教学法》。实用主义教育学的主要观点。

(4) 批判教育学　[美]鲍尔斯与金蒂斯的《资本主义美国的学校教育》、[法]布迪厄的《教育、社会和文化的再生产》、[美]阿普尔的《教育与权力》、[美]吉鲁的《批判教育学、国家与文化斗争》。批判教育学的主要观点。

5. 当代教育学理论的新发展

苏联教育家赞科夫的《教学与发展》，提出以高难度进行教学、以高速度进行教学、理论知识起主导作用、使学生理解学习过程、使全班学生包括差生都得到一般发展的五条教学原则，教学与发展的关系。巴拉诺夫的《教育学》、巴班斯基的《教学过程最优化》、阿莫纳什维利的《合作教育学》以及苏霍姆林斯基的《给教师的建议》《把整个心灵献给儿童》。

美国心理学家布卢姆制定出的新的教育目标分类系统，他把教育目标分为认知领域目标、情感领域目标和动作技能领域目标三大类。美国教育家布鲁纳的《教育过程》，提出“结构主义学说”和“发现法”的教学方法。德国教育家瓦·根舍因提出“范例方式教学理论”；瑞士教育家皮亚杰的《教育科学与儿童心理学》，提出儿童思维发展阶段等理论。

二十世纪七十年代，法国的保尔·朗格朗在其《终身教育引论》中提出了“终身教育”和“学习化社会”的概念。终身教育思想在当代教育理论和实践中引起了广泛的重视。

（三）学习教育学的意义

1. 有助于树立正确的教育思想，提高贯彻我国社会主义教育方针、政策的自觉性。

2. 有助于巩固热爱教育事业的专业思想，全面提高教师的素养。

3. 有助于认识和掌握教育规律，提高从事学校教育教学工作的水平和能力。

4. 有助于推动学校教育教学改革和教育科学研究。

二、教育的本质、功能和基本规律

【要求】

1. 识记教育、遗传、环境、教育功能的概念，教育的本质属性和社会属性，各个社会历史时期教育的目的、内容。

2. 理解和掌握教育的基本规律；识别不同的教育功能观和教育功能的类型。

3. 能运用上述基本原理分析和说明有关教育现象和问题。

（一）教育的本质

1. 教育的基本概念

（1）广义的概念

泛指一切有目的地增进人的知识和技能、发展人的智力和体力、影响人的思想品德的活动。其中包括社会教育、学校教育和家庭教育。

（2）狭义的概念

指学校教育，是教育者按一定社会（或阶级）的要求和受教育者身心发展的规律，对受教育者所进行的一种有目的、有计划、有组织的系统影响的社会活动。

狭义的教育有时可以作为思想品德教育的同义语使用。

2. 教育的属性

(1) 教育的本质属性

教育是有目的的培养人的社会实践活动。

(2) 教育的社会属性

① 教育具有永恒性。教育是人类特有的社会现象,它与人类社会相始终,它是一个永恒的范畴。

② 教育具有历史性。教育又是一个历史的范畴,不同的历史时期有不同的教育,在阶级社会表现为鲜明的阶级性。

③ 教育具有相对的独立性。具体表现在:教育具有自身的继承关系;教育要受其他社会意识形态的影响;教育与社会政治经济发展不平衡。教育的独立性是相对的,不能将其绝对化。

3. 教育的起源和发展

(1) 教育的起源

① 教育的神话起源说;② 以法国利托尔诺为代表的教育生物起源说;③ 以美国孟禄为代表的教育心理起源说;④ 马克思主义的劳动起源说。

(2) 教育的发展

① 原始社会教育的基本特征:教育的社会性和无阶级性;教育和社会生活、生产劳动融合在一起;言传身教和模仿是教育的主要手段。

② 古代社会的教育,包括奴隶社会和封建社会的教育。

我国奴隶社会学校名称——“庠”“序”“校”等,教育目的是培养大小奴隶主,教育内容是六艺——礼、乐、射、御、书、数。欧洲奴隶社会曾出现过两种著名的教育体系——斯巴达教育和雅典教育。前者注重培养军人和武士,教育内容主要是军事体育;后者则重视培养多方面发展的人,教育内容包括文法、修辞、哲学、科学、艺术、体操等许多方面,提倡“缪司”教育。

我国封建社会的教育目的是培养各级封建官吏,教育内容主要是儒家的经典——“四书五经”。欧洲封建社会的两种教育体系——教会教育和骑士教育,前者的教育目的是培养教士和僧侣,教育内容是七艺,包括三科(文法、修辞、辩证法),四学(算术、几何、天文、音乐),但各科都贯穿神学;后者的教育目的是培养勇猛善战的封建骑士,教育内容是骑士七技，包括骑马、游泳、投枪、击剑、打猎、下棋、吟诗。

③ 现代社会的教育，包括资本主义社会的教育和社会主义社会的教育。

资本主义社会教育的概况：资本主义教育较之封建教育进行的改革，在教育目的上，出现了双重的培养目标；在教育内容上，增加了大量的自然科学知识；在教学方法上，出现了实验、演示、实习等新的教学方法；在教学组织形式上，以班级授课制代替了个别教学，第一次提出了普及义务教育的问题。

社会主义教育的特点：教育权为广大劳动人民所掌握，教育为社会主义服务，为人民服务；共产党统一领导、创办；以马克思主义为指导，提倡唯物主义，反对宗教迷信；全社会实施平等的民族教育，反对民族压迫；教育与生产劳动相结合，是培养全面发展的人的唯一方法。

4. 教育的功能

(1) 教育功能的概念：教育功能是教育活动、教育系统对个体、社会发展所产生的各种影响和作用。

(2) 教育功能的类型

① 从作用的对象划分，可分为教育的个体功能和社会功能。

② 从作用的方向划分，可分为教育的正向功能和负向功能。

③ 从作用的呈现形式划分，可分为教育的显性功能和隐性功能。

④ 从作用的性质划分，可以分为教育的本体功能和派生功能。

(3) 教育的个体功能

教育促进个体生理发展的功能；教育促进个体心理发展的功能。

(4) 教育的社会功能

教育的政治功能；教育的经济功能；教育的文化功能，包括传递与保存文化、活化文化、交流与融合文化、选择文化、更新与创造文化的功能；教育的生态功能；教育的人口功能等。

(二) 教育的基本规律

1. 教育与社会发展相互制约的规律

(1) 教育与生产力相互制约

① 生产力对教育的制约作用：生产力对教育目的、教育内容、教育

发展的规模和速度、学校结构、教学方法和手段、教学组织形式的制约。

② 教育对生产力的促进作用：教育是劳动力再生产的必要手段；教育是科学知识和技术再生产的手段；教育是生产新的科学知识和技术的手段。

（2）教育与社会政治经济制度相互制约

① 社会政治经济制度对教育的制约作用：社会政治经济制度对教育性质、教育目的、教育的领导权和受教育权、某些教育内容等方面的制约。

② 教育对社会政治经济制度的反作用：教育培养出具有一定阶级意识的人，维护和巩固一定的社会政治经济制度；教育通过影响社会舆论、道德风尚为政治经济制度服务；教育对社会政治经济制度不起决定作用。

2. 教育与人的发展相互制约的规律

（1）影响人的发展的主要因素

① 遗传的概念；遗传在人的发展中的作用。

② 环境的概念和组成；环境在人的发展中的作用；人对环境的反映是能动的反映。

③ 教育对人的发展的制约：教育在人的发展中起主导作用。其原因是：教育是一种有目的的培养人的活动，它规定着人的发展方向；教育，特别是学校教育给人的影响比较全面、系统和深刻；学校有专门负责教育工作的教师。

（2）人的发展对教育的制约

① 教育要适应人的发展的顺序性和阶段性，循序渐进地促进人的发展。

② 教育要适应人的发展的不均衡性，在人的身心发展的某一关键期，施以相应的教育。

③ 教育要适应人的发展的稳定性和可变性，既考虑稳定性，不任意改动教育内容和方法，又注意可变性，充分挖掘受教育者的发展潜力。

④ 教育要适应人的发展的个别差异性，做到因材施教。

三、教育目的

【要求】

1. 识记教育目的、德育、智育、体育、美育、劳动教育、素质教育等概念以及新中国成立后我国各个历史时期的教育方针。

2. 理解和掌握智育、体育、美育、劳动教育的意义、目的、任务、内容、实施的组织形式和途径。

3. 明确有关教育目的的理论、马克思关于人的全面发展学说，理解素质教育的意义。能以本章的理论分析和说明教育实践中存在和出现的有关热点问题。

（一）教育目的的意义

1. 教育目的和培养目标的概念

教育目的是教育主体对于其所希望达到的教育结果的设定，是培养人的质量规格要求。培养目标是教育目的的具体化，是结合教育目的、社会要求和受教育者的特点制定的各级各类教育或专业的培养要求。

2. 教育目的的意义

（1）教育目的既是教育工作的出发点，也是教育工作的归宿。

（2）教育目的对提高教育质量具有指导意义。

（二）确立教育目的的依据

1. 马克思关于人的全面发展学说

（1）人的全面发展的含义。最根本的是指人的劳动能力，即人的体力和智力的全面、和谐、充分的发展。

（2）造成人的片面发展的原因。其根本原因是旧式分工所导致的城乡分离、脑体分离。

（3）机器大工业生产提供了人的全面发展的基础和可能，但资本主义制度阻碍了人的全面发展的历史进步趋势。

（4）社会主义制度是实现人的全面发展的社会条件，教育与生产劳动相结合是培养全面发展的人的唯一方法。

2. 社会生产方式

（1）教育目的的确立受社会生产力制约。

(2) 教育目的的确立也受一定的生产关系和以这种生产关系为基础的政治观点、政治制度的制约。

3. 人的自身发展需要

教育目的的确立还应考虑人的兴趣、爱好、性格、能力等个性发展的需求。

4. 有关教育目的确立的理论

(1) 个人本位论及其主要观点

① 教育目的是根据个人的发展需要而制定的。

② 个人价值高于社会价值,社会价值只是表现在它有助于个人发展。

③ 人生来就具有健全的本能,教育目的就在于促使本能不受影响地发展。

(2) 社会本位论及其主要观点

① 个人的一切发展都有赖于社会。

② 教育除社会目的外,无其他目的。

③ 教育结果只能用社会效益加以衡量,看它为社会贡献了什么。

(三) 我国的教育目的

1. 我国社会主义教育目的的基本点

(1) 培养社会主义建设者和接班人,表明了我国社会主义教育目的的性质和方向。

(2) 德、智、体、美、劳全面发展,是我国社会主义教育目的中对受教育者的素质要求。

(3) 教育与生产劳动和社会实践相结合,是实现我国社会主义教育目的的根本途径。

2. 我国的教育方针

(1) 1950 年颁布的教育方针

(2) 1957 年颁布的教育方针

(3) 1958 年颁布的教育方针

(4) 1981 年颁布的教育方针

(5) 2021 年颁布的教育方针

坚持教育必须为社会主义现代化建设服务，为人民服务，必须与生产劳动和社会实践相结合，培养德智体美劳全面发展的社会主义建设者和接班人。

3. 素质教育

（1）素质教育的内涵

① 以提高国民素质为根本宗旨。

② 是面向全体学生的教育。

③ 具有全面性、主体性和可持续性。

④ 是促进学生个性发展的教育。

⑤ 要着力提高学生的社会责任感、创新精神和社会实践能力。

（2）素质教育的意义

① 素质教育有助于提高中华民族的整体素质，提高综合国力。

② 素质教育是克服应试教育的弊端，深化教育改革的必然趋势。

③ 素质教育是实施全面发展教育的具体落实。

（四）全面发展教育的组成部分

1. 德育（详见“八、德育理论与实践”）

2. 智育

（1）智育的意义

① 智育在社会物质文明和精神文明建设中起着不可缺少的越来越重要的作用。

② 智育在全面发展教育中处于十分重要的地位，它是全面发展教育的基础和核心。

（2）智育的任务

① 让学生掌握系统的科学文化基础知识和基本技能技巧。

② 发展学生的智力。智力的概念、发展智力的原因、智力与能力的区别。

③ 培养学生良好的学习品质和热爱科学的精神。

3. 体育

（1）体育的概念

体育是以身体活动为基本内容，促进人的身心发展，培育人、塑造人的过程。

(2) 体育的意义

① 促进学生身体健康发展,增强学生的体质。

② 体育是促进学生全面发展不可缺少的条件,为学生全面发展提供物质基础。

③ 青少年一代的身心健康水平,关系国家、民族的强弱盛衰。

(3) 体育的任务

体育的根本任务是增强学生的体质。具体任务包括:

① 促使学生正常发育和身体各器官机能的发展,全面发展学生的身体素质和人体基本活动能力,提高适应环境的能力。

② 向学生传授体育和卫生的基本知识和基本技能,养成科学锻炼身体的习惯。

③ 通过体育对学生进行思想品德教育。

④ 向国家输送优秀体育运动员,促进我国体育运动水平的提高。

(4) 体育的内容

田径、体操、球类、游戏、游泳、武术、军事体育(国防体育)。

(5) 体育的组织形式

基本组织形式是体育课。其他形式有:早操、课间操;课外体育锻炼;运动队训练;运动竞赛。

4. 美育

(1) 美育的概念

美育是通过现实美和艺术美来打动学生的感情,使学生在心灵深处受到感染和感化,从而培养学生正确的审美观点,具有感受美、鉴赏美、表现美和创造美的能力的教育。

(2) 美育对促进学生全面发展的意义

① 美育能促进学生智力发展,扩大和加深学生对客观现实的认识。

② 美育能促进学生科学世界观和共产主义道德品质的形成。

③ 美育能促进体育,美育具有怡情健身的作用。

④ 美育能促进劳动教育,使学生体验到劳动创造美的喜悦。

（3）美育的任务

① 培养学生正确的审美观，使学生具有感受美、鉴赏美的知识和能力。

② 培养学生表现美、创造美的能力。

③ 培养学生的心灵美和行为美。

（4）美育的实施途径

① 通过各科教学和课外文艺活动实施美育。

② 通过大自然实施美育。

③ 通过社会日常生活实施美育。

5. 劳动教育

（1）劳动教育的内涵和意义

劳动教育是发挥劳动的育人功能，对学生进行热爱劳动、热爱劳动人民的教育活动。

实施劳动教育的重点是在系统的文化知识学习之外，有目的、有计划地组织学生参加日常生活劳动、生产劳动和服务性劳动，让学生动手实践、出力流汗，接受锻炼、磨炼意志，培养学生正确劳动价值观和良好劳动品质。

① 劳动教育是中国特色社会主义教育制度的重要内容，是全面发展教育体系的重要内容，是大中小学必须开展的教育活动。

② 劳动教育是学生成长的必要途径，具有树德、增智、强体、育美的综合育人价值。

③ 有利于完成升学和就业双重任务，适应社会主义现代化建设的需要。

（2）劳动教育的目标

全面提高学生劳动素养，使学生：

① 树立正确的劳动观念。

② 具有必备的劳动能力。

③ 培育积极的劳动精神。

④ 养成良好的劳动习惯和品质。

（3）劳动教育的内容

① 日常生活劳动。

② 生产劳动。

③ 服务性劳动。

(4) 劳动教育的途径

① 独立开设劳动教育必修课。

② 在学科专业中有机渗透劳动教育。

③ 在课外校外活动中安排劳动实践。

④ 在校园文化建设中强化劳动文化。

四、教育制度

【要求】

1. 识记教育制度的概念,现代学制的主要类型和建立学制的依据。

2. 掌握我国现代学制的沿革概况,主要指现代学制颁布的年代、名称及有关规定。

3. 理解我国基本教育制度以及学制进一步改革的原则。

(一) 教育制度的概述

1. 教育制度的概念

(1) 广义概念

指国民教育制度,是一个国家为实现其国民教育目的,从组织系统上建立起来的一切教育设施和有关制度。

(2) 狭义概念

指学校教育制度,简称学制,是一个国家各级各类学校的总体系,具体规定各级各类学校的性质、任务、目的、要求、入学条件、学制年限及它们之间的相互关系。

2. 现代学制的类型

(1) 以英国为代表的双轨学制

(2) 以美国为代表的单轨学制

(3) 以苏联为代表的分支式学制

3. 建立学制的依据

(1) 生产力水平和科学技术状况

(2) 社会政治经济制度

(3) 青少年身心发展规律

(4) 本国学制的历史发展和国外学制的影响

（二）我国现代学制的沿革

1. 旧中国的学制

(1) 1902 年颁布“壬寅学制”(未实行)

(2) 1903 年颁布“癸卯学制”(实行新学制的开始)

(3) 1912 年颁布“壬子癸丑学制”

(4) 1922 年颁布“壬戌学制”(又称新学制，六三三制，以美国学制为蓝本)

2. 新中国的学制改革

(1) 1951 年颁布中华人民共和国新学制

(2) 1958 年的学制改革

确定了“两条腿走路”的办学方针和“三个结合”“六个并举”的具体办学原则。

(3) 1985 年颁布《中共中央关于教育体制改革的决定》

① 改革的根本目的是提高中华民族素质，多出人才，出好人才。

② 把普及九年制义务教育的责任交给地方，有计划、有步骤地普及九年制义务教育。

③ 中等教育改革。

④ 高等教育改革。

⑤ 加强领导，保证改革顺利进行。

(4) 1993 年颁布《中国教育改革和发展纲要》

其中有关教育制度的内容：

① 确定了 20 世纪末教育发展的总目标。

② 调整中等教育结构。

③ 改革办学体制。

④ 改革高校的招生和毕业生分配制度。

⑤ 改革和完善教育投资体制。

(5) 2004 年的《2003—2007 年教育振兴行动计划》

其中有关教育制度的内容：

① 努力提高普及九年制义务教育的水平和质量，为 2010 年全面普及九年制义务教育和全面提高义务教育质量打好基础。

② 深化农村教育改革，发展农村职业教育和成人教育，推进“三教统筹”和“农科教”结合。

③ 落实“以县为主”的农村义务教育管理体制，加大投入，保障完善机制。

④ 建立和健全助学制度，扶持农村家庭经济困难学生接受义务教育。

⑤ 以全面推进素质教育为目标，加快考试评价制度改革。

⑥ 积极推进普通高中、学前教育和特殊教育的改革与发展。

⑦ 大力发展职业教育、多样化的成人教育和继续教育。

⑧ 健全教育督导与评估体系，保障教育发展与改革目标的实现。

⑨ 深化学校内部管理体制改革，探索建立现代学校制度。

(6) 2021 年修订《中华人民共和国教育法》

我国基本教育制度：

① 学校教育制度。

② 九年制义务教育制度。

③ 职业教育制度和继续教育制度。

④ 国家教育考试制度。

⑤ 学业证书制度。

⑥ 学位制度。

⑦ 扫除文盲的教育制度。

⑧ 教育督导制度和学校及其他教育机构教育评估制度。

(7) 我国学制进一步改革的基本原则

① 教育结构必须适应经济结构和社会结构。

② 统一性与多样性相结合。

③ 普及与提高相结合。

④ 稳定性与灵活性相结合。

五、教师与学生

【要求】

1. 识记教师的作用和任务，学生身心发展的特点。

2. 理解教师劳动的特点，学生的权利和义务，学生在教育过程中的地位和作用，以及师生关系。

3. 掌握教师应具备的素养以及教师专业发展的概念、内容和途径。

（一）教师

1. 教师的作用

（1）教师对社会发展的作用

（2）教师对青少年成长的作用

（3）教师在教育工作中的作用

2. 教师的任务

教师的根本任务是教书育人。

3. 教师劳动的特点

（1）复杂性、创造性

（2）主体性、示范性

（3）长期性、连续性

（4）间接性、广延性

4. 教师的专业素养

（1）职业道德素养

① 爱岗敬业；② 热爱学生；③ 团结协作；④ 为人师表。

（2）知识素养

① 政治理论知识；② 学科专业知识；③ 文化基础知识；④ 教育科学知识。

（3）能力素养

① 语言表达能力；② 教育教学管理能力；③ 教育教学的组织能力；④ 自我反思能力。

5. 教师专业发展

(1) 教师专业发展的概念

教师专业发展是指教师作为专业人员，在专业思想、专业知识、专业能力等方面不断完善的过程，即由一个专业新手逐渐发展成为一个专家型教师的过程。

(2) 教师专业发展的内容

① 专业理想的建立；② 专业知识的拓展与深化；③ 专业能力的提高；④ 专业自我的形成。

(3) 教师专业发展的途径

主要是建立一个开放的、灵活的、职前职后一体化的教师教育体系。具体包括：师范教育；新教师的入职辅导和教师在职培训；教师资格证书制度；教学反思与研究。

(二) 学生

1. 学生身心发展的特点

(1) 学生是自我教育和发展的主体

① 依据；② 表现。

(2) 学生是教育的对象

① 依据；② 表现。

(3) 学生是发展中的人

① 学生年龄特征的概念。

② 学生的年龄分期。

婴儿期(又称先学前期，相当于托儿所阶段)——出生至三岁；

幼儿期(又称学前期，相当于幼儿园阶段)——三岁至五六岁；

童年期(又称学龄初期，相当于小学阶段)——五六岁至十一二岁；

少年期(又称学龄中期，相当于初中阶段)——十一二岁至十四五岁；

青年初期(又称学龄晚期，相当于高中阶段)——十四五岁至十七八岁。

2. 学生的权利与义务

(1)《教育法》对学生权利的规定

① 参加教育教学计划安排的各种活动，使用教育教学设施、设备、图书资料。

② 按照国家的有关规定获得奖学金、贷学金、助学金。

③ 在学业成绩和品行上获得公正评价，完成规定的学业后获得相应的学业证书、学位证书。

④ 对学校给予的处分不服，向有关部门提出申诉，对学校、教师侵犯其人身权、财产权等合法权益提出申诉或者依法提起诉讼。

⑤ 法律、法规规定的其他权利。包括：受教育权、姓名权、荣誉权、隐私权和健康权。

（2）《教育法》对学生义务的规定

① 遵守法律、法规。

② 遵守学生行为规范，尊敬师长，养成良好的思想品德和行为习惯。

③ 努力学习，完成规定的学习任务。

④ 遵守其所在学校或者其他教育机构的管理制度和规定。

（三）师生关系

1. 师生关系的概述

2. 我国新型师生关系的特点

（1）尊师爱生

（2）民主平等

（3）教学相长

3. 师生关系的建立与发展

（1）师生关系的含义

（2）师生关系的作用

（3）师生关系的基本类型

（4）师生关系的建立与发展

① 树立正确的学生观；② 提高教师自身素养；③ 掌握师生沟通艺术。

六、课程

【要求】

1. 识记课程的概念。掌握课程的要素、内容及表现形式，课程的类型。

2. 理解课程的意义，制定义务教育课程方案的基本原则，国内外课程改革的趋势，我国基础教育课程改革的目标、特点等内容。

3. 能运用有关的课程理论解释和分析学校课程实践问题。

（一）课程概述

1. 课程的概念

（1）广义的课程

学校为实现培养目标而选择的教育内容及其进程的总和，它包括学校老师所教授的各门学科和有目的、有计划的教育活动。

（2）狭义的课程

学生在学校学习的某一门学科、应该从事的活动内容及其有计划的进程。

2. 课程的意义

（1）实现教育教学目标的保证

（2）设计教育教学活动的依据

（3）实施教育教学活动的中介

（4）评价教育教学效果的标准

（二）课程的要素、内容和类型

1. 课程的要素

（1）课程目标

（2）课程内容

（3）课程结构

（4）课程设计

课程设计的两大基本模式：以泰勒为代表的目标模式和以斯滕豪斯为代表的过程模式。

（5）课程评价

2. 课程的内容及表现形式

（1）课程的内容

① 关于自然、社会和人的发展规律的基础知识。

② 关于一般智力技能和操作技能的知识经验。

③ 关于对待世界与他人的态度的知识经验。

（2）课程的具体表现形式

在我国，课程主要由三部分组成，即课程方案、课程标准和教材。

① 课程方案

课程方案是根据教育目的和不同类型学校的教育任务，由国家教育主管部门制定的有关教学和教育工作的指导性文件。

课程方案包括培养目标、基本原则、课程标准编制与教材编写、课程实施等。

制定义务教育课程方案的基本原则：坚持全面发展，育人为本；面向全体学生，因材施教；聚焦核心素养，面向未来；加强课程综合，注重关联；变革育人方式，突出实践。

② 课程标准

课程标准是指根据课程方案以纲要形式编定的有关课程教学内容的指导性文件，它规定了各门课程的性质、理念、目标、内容、学业质量、实施建议等。

③ 教材

教材是知识授受活动中的主要信息媒介，是依据课程标准编制的教学规范用书。教材可以是印刷品，也可以是音像制品、软件等。

编写课程标准和教材应遵循的原则是：思想性和科学性的统一；理论联系实际；稳定性和时代性相结合；系统性和可接受性。

3. 课程的类型

（1）从课程管理制度角度划分

① 国家课程；② 地方课程；③ 校本课程。

（2）从课程的组织形式划分

① 学科课程；② 活动课程。

（3）从学生对课程选择的自由度划分

① 必修课程；② 选修课程。

（4）从课程的存在形式划分

① 显性课程；② 隐性课程。

（三）课程改革

1. 国外课程改革的基本趋势

(1) 追求卓越的整体性课程目标

(2) 重视课程内容的现代化

(3) 提倡多样化的课程结构

(4) 加强普通教育和职业教育的课程融合

(5) 加大课程难度,进行“尖子生”的筛选和培养

2. 我国于2001年开始的基础教育课程改革

(1) 我国基础教育课程改革的目标

① 课程任务方面的改革目标;② 课程结构方面的改革目标;③ 课程内容方面的改革目标;④ 课程实施方面的改革目标;⑤ 课程评价方面的改革目标;⑥ 课程管理方面的改革目标。

(2) 我国基础教育课程设置的特点

① 小学阶段以综合课程为主;初中阶段分科课程与综合课程相结合;高中阶段则以分科课程为主。

② 从小学到高中设置综合实践活动课,并作为必修课程。综合实践活动是从学生的真实生活和发展需要出发,从生活情境中发现问题、转化为活动主题,通过探究、服务、制作、体验等方式,培养学生综合素质的跨学科实践性课程。

③ 农村中学课程强调为当地社会经济发展服务。

④ 在课程标准方面,也提出了一些适应我国当前国情的新要求。

七、教学理论与实践

【要求】

1. 识记教学、教学过程、教学原则、教学方法、教学手段、班级授课制、小组教学等概念。

2. 理解和掌握教学过程的本质和规律、教学原则、教学方法及其改革、教学模式、教学基本环节、教学评价等内容。

3. 能运用教学过程的规律、教学原则等解释说明有关教学实践的具体问题。

(一) 教学概述

1. 教学的概念

教学是教师的教和学生的学共同组成的传递和掌握社会经验的双边活动。

2. 教学的地位与作用

教学是学校的中心工作，学校工作必须坚持“教学为主、全面安排”的原则。教学是实现教育目的的基本途径。

3. 教学的基本任务

（1）传授与学习学科基础知识与基本技能

（2）发展学生的智能，特别是培养学生的创新精神与实践能力

（3）发展学生的体力，提高学生的身心健康水平

（4）培养学生的审美情趣和能力

（5）发展学生积极的情感、态度和价值观，形成良好品德和个性心理品质

（二）教学过程

1. 教学过程的概念

教学过程是教师根据一定的社会要求和学生身心发展的特点，引导学生有目的、有计划地掌握系统的文化科学基础知识和基本技能，同时身心获得发展，形成一定思想品德的过程。

2. 教学过程的本质

教学过程是一种特殊的认识过程，是以认识过程为基础，促进学生发展的过程。

3. 教学过程的基本规律

（1）间接经验与直接经验相结合的规律

（2）教师主导作用与学生主体作用相统一的规律

（3）掌握知识与发展智力相统一的规律

（4）知识教学与品德教育相统一的规律（教学的教育性规律）

4. 教学过程的基本阶段

（1）激发学习动机

（2）感知教材

（3）理解教材

(4) 巩固知识

(5) 运用知识

(6) 检查知识、技能和技巧

(三) 教学原则

1. 教学原则的概念

教学原则是有效地进行教学必须遵循的基本要求，是指导教学工作的一般原理。

2. 教学原则与教学规律的区别与联系

教学规律是教学内部的本质联系，是客观的；教学原则是第二性的，是人们制定的。教学原则是教学规律在教学中的反映；不同的教学体系有不同的教学原则。

3. 我国目前基本的教学原则及其运用

(1) 科学性与教育性相结合原则

① 基本含义；② 贯彻此原则的基本要求。

(2) 理论联系实际原则

① 基本含义；② 贯彻此原则的基本要求。

(3) 直观性原则

① 基本含义；② 贯彻此原则的基本要求。

(4) 启发性原则

① 基本含义；② 贯彻此原则的基本要求。

(5) 循序渐进原则

① 基本含义；② 贯彻此原则的基本要求。

(6) 巩固性原则

① 基本含义；② 贯彻此原则的基本要求。

(7) 因材施教原则

① 基本含义；② 贯彻此原则的基本要求。

(四) 教学方法

1. 教学方法的概述

(1) 教学方法的概念

教学方法是教师和学生为实现教育目的、完成教学任务所采用的手段和一整套工作方式。

(2) 教学方法的意义

(3) 两种对立的教学方法指导思想

① 启发式;② 注入式。

2. 常用的教学方法

(1) 以语言传递为主的教学方法

① 讲授法:包括讲述、讲解、讲读、讲演等;② 谈话法;③ 讨论法;④ 读书指导法。

(2) 以直观感知为主的教学方法

① 演示法;② 参观法。

(3) 以实际训练为主的教学方法

① 练习法;② 实验法;③ 实习作业法;④ 实践活动法。

(4) 以探究活动为主的教学方法,如发现法等

(5) 以情感陶冶(体验)为主的教学方法

① 欣赏教学法;② 情境教学法。

3. 教学方法的改革趋势

(1) 由以教为中心走向以学为中心

(2) 由单一化走向多样化

(3) 由孤立走向整合

(4) 重视以问题为导向

(5) 与现代信息技术深度融合

4. 学生的学习方式

(1) 接受学习与研究性学习的概念

(2) 研究性学习的目的与意义

(3) 接受学习与研究性学习的比较

5. 教学方法的选择与运用

(1) 选择教学方法的依据

① 教学任务;② 教学内容;③ 学生年龄特征;④ 教师自身特点。

(2) 教学方法运用的综合性、灵活性、创造性

(五) 教学手段

1. 教学手段的概念

2. 教学手段的演变阶段

① 口耳相传；② 文字教材；③ 直观教具；④ 电教工具；⑤ 计算机与多媒体；⑥ 网络教学。

3. 现代化教学手段在教学中的作用

(1) 教材建设的突破

(2) 教学组织形式的突破

(3) 师生关系的突破

(4) 提高了教学质量和教学效率

(5) 扩大了教学规模

4. 现代化教学手段的发展趋势

(1) 教学媒体日益自动化、微型化

(2) 新的教学媒体不断涌现

(3) 教学手段运用的多媒体化、综合化和网络化

(4) 现代化教学的服务目标多样化

(六) 教学组织形式

1. 教学组织形式的概念

2. 教学组织形式的类型

(1) 班级授课

① 概念；② 意义；③ 改革。

(2) 分组教学

① 概念；② 意义；③ 要求。

(3) 个别教学

① 概念；② 意义；③ 要求。

(4) 现场教学

① 概念；② 意义；③ 要求。

(5) 复式教学

① 概念；② 意义；③ 要求。

(七) 教学模式

1. 教学模式的概念

教学模式是在一定教学理论或教学思想指导下，通过教学实践抽象概括而形成的相对稳定的教学活动基本结构或范型。

2. 教学模式的特点

（1）完整性；（2）简约性；（3）操作性；（4）针对性。

3. 教学模式的要素

（1）主题；（2）目标；（3）策略；（4）程序；（5）评价。

4. 常见的教学模式

（1）讲授-接受模式

（2）自学辅导模式

（3）探究模式

（4）陶冶模式

（八）教学工作的基本环节

1. 备课

（1）备课的意义

（2）备课的要求

① 做好三方面的工作：了解学生、钻研教材、设计教法；② 写好三种计划：学年（或学期）教学进度计划、单元（或课题）计划、课时计划（教案）。

2. 上课

（1）上课的意义

（2）一堂好课的基本标准

① 教师教的标准：教学目的明确；内容正确；结构合理；方法恰当；语言艺术；板书有序；教态从容自如。

② 学生学的标准：学生注意力集中；思维活跃；积极参与；充分发挥自身特长。

3. 课外作业的布置与反馈

（1）课外作业的意义

（2）课外作业的形式

① 阅读教科书和参考书；② 各种口头作业和口头问答；③ 各种书面作业；④ 各种实践作业。

(3) 作业布置的基本要求

① 作业内容符合课程标准的要求;② 作业考虑不同学生的能力与需求;③ 作业分量适宜,难易适度;④ 作业形式多样,具有多选性;⑤ 作业要求明确,规定完成时间;⑥ 作业反馈清晰、及时。

4. 课外辅导

(1) 课外辅导的意义

(2) 课外辅导的内容

① 给学生解答疑难问题,指导学生做好作业;② 为基础差和因事、因病缺课的学生补课;③ 给成绩特别优异的学生做个别辅导;④ 给学生学习方法上的辅导;⑤ 对学生进行学习目的和学习态度的教育。

(3) 课外辅导的基本要求

① 从辅导对象实际出发确定辅导内容和措施;② 辅导只是对课堂教学的补充,不能将主要精力放在辅导上。

5. 学业成绩检查与评定

(1) 学业成绩检查与评定的意义

(2) 学业成绩检查的方式

① 平时考查;② 考试(包括期中考试、期末考试和毕业考试)。方式有口试、笔试和实践考核。

(3) 学业成绩检查的基本要求

① 根据教学目标制定评价标准;② 编制测验蓝图。

(4) 成绩评定的方法

① 百分制记分法;② 等级制记分法。

(5) 学业成绩评定的基本要求

① 客观公正;② 向学生指出学习上的优缺点和努力方向。

(九) 教学评价及其改革

1. 教学评价的概念

教学评价是指以教学目标为依据,通过一定的标准和手段,对教学活动及其结果给予价值上的判断。

2. 教学评价的意义

3. 教学评价的原则

(1) 客观性;(2) 全面性;(3) 指导性;(4) 科学性。

4. 教学评价的类型

(1) 诊断性评价;(2) 形成性评价;(3) 终结性评价。

5. 教学评价的改革

重视形成性评价和如何促进学生发展方面的评价。

八、德育理论与实践

【要求】

1. 识记德育、德育过程、各种德育方法的概念以及德育内容。

2. 理解和掌握德育过程的规律、德育原则和德育途径的主要内容。

3. 能运用德育过程规律、德育原则,解释、说明有关德育实践的具体问题。

(一) 德育的概述

1. 德育的概念

德育是教育者根据受教育者身心发展规律,有目的、有计划地培养受教育者品德的活动。它一般包括政治教育、思想教育和道德品质教育三个基本方面。

道德与品德的区别与联系;道德与法律的区别与联系。

2. 德育的重要意义

(1) 德育是进行社会主义精神文明建设和物质文明建设的重要条件

(2) 德育在青少年思想品德的形成与发展中起着主导作用,是培养社会主义新人的条件

(3) 德育是学校全面发展教育的基本组成部分,是实现教育目的的重要保证

3. 德育的任务

我国中小学德育总的任务是把全体学生培养成为爱国的,具有社会公德、文明行为习惯的遵纪守法的好公民。

具体任务是：

（1）培养学生初步树立坚定正确的政治方向

（2）引导学生逐步确立科学的世界观和人生观

（3）逐步使学生养成社会主义的基本道德、法纪观念和文明行为习惯

（4）培养学生具有一定的品德能力和良好的品德心理品质

（二）德育的内容

1. 爱国主义教育

2. 理想教育

3. 集体主义教育

4. 劳动教育

5. 自觉纪律教育

6. 民主和法制教育

7. 科学世界观和人生观教育

8. 道德教育

9. 生态教育

（三）德育过程

1. 德育过程的概念

德育过程是教育者根据一定社会的德育要求和受教育者品德形成发展的规律，把一定社会的道德规范转化为受教育者品德的过程。

2. 德育过程与思想品德形成过程的区别与联系

德育过程的根本目的在于促进人的思想品德的形成和发展，是师生共同活动的实施过程；思想品德形成过程是受教育者自身的道德认识、道德情感、道德意志、道德行为习惯的发展过程。二者之间既有区别，又有联系，互为条件。

3. 德育过程的基本矛盾

德育过程的基本矛盾是教育者提出的德育要求与受教育者已有的品德基础的矛盾。

4. 德育过程的基本规律

（1）德育过程是对学生知、情、意、行的培养提高过程。

(2) 德育过程是促进学生思想内部矛盾斗争的发展过程。

(3) 德育过程是组织学生的活动和交往、统一多方面教育影响的过程。

(4) 德育过程是一个长期的、反复的、逐步提高的过程。

(四) 德育的基本原则

1. 现实性与方向性相结合的原则

(1) 基本含义

(2) 贯彻此原则的要求

2. 从学生实际出发的原则

(1) 基本含义

(2) 贯彻此原则的要求

3. 知行统一的原则

(1) 基本含义

(2) 贯彻此原则的要求

4. 集体教育与个别教育相结合的原则

(1) 基本含义

(2) 贯彻此原则的要求

5. 正面教育与纪律约束相结合的原则

(1) 基本含义

(2) 贯彻此原则的要求

6. 依靠积极因素克服消极因素的原则(又称长善救失的原则)

(1) 基本含义

(2) 贯彻此原则的要求

7. 尊重信任学生与严格要求学生相结合的原则

(1) 基本含义

(2) 贯彻此原则的要求

8. 教育影响的一致性和连贯性原则

(1) 基本含义

(2) 贯彻此原则的要求

(五) 德育的途径和方法

1. 德育的途径

(1) 校内正式途径

① 教学;② 共青团、少先队组织的活动及课外活动;③ 校会、班会、周会、晨会、时事政策学习;④ 班主任工作;⑤ 劳动教育、美育活动、体育活动。

(2) 校内非正式途径

① 学生友谊团体;② 校园文化氛围。

(3) 校外正式途径

① 校外教育;② 社会实践活动;③ 社区文化教育机构;④ 家庭教育。

(4) 校外非正式途径

① 邻里;② 非正式社会、文化团体。

2. 德育方法的选择与运用

(1) 常用的德育方法

① 说理教育法;② 榜样示范法;③ 实际锻炼法;④ 陶冶教育法;⑤ 指导自我教育法;⑥ 品德评价法。

(2) 德育方法的选择依据

① 德育目标;② 德育内容;③ 德育对象的年龄特点和个性差异。

(3) 德育方法的改革

① 双导法:又称启发诱导法。是说服教育的一种,即从正反两个方面教育引导学生提高认识,形成良好思想品德的方法。

② 疏导法:即开导、引导、诱导的方法。指教育者启发学生祛除思想和心理障碍,因势利导,提高学生思想品德的方法。

③ 对话法:指教育者与学生集体或个体交谈,以解答学生提出的质疑为目的的谈话方法。

④ 感化法:是动之以情的方法。即教育者以真心诚意的关怀、尊重、信任来触动学生心灵,感化学生,使其提高思想品德的方法。

⑤ 交流法:指教育者创设交往情境,提供社会互动机会,组织多方面交往活动来教育学生的方法。

⑥ 心理咨询法:指通过询问解答的方式,帮助学生消除影响他们

思想品德形成和发展的心理障碍，进而培养学生思想品德的方法。

3. 德育工作的新形式

(1) 通过开展社区教育进行德育

(2) 创办业余党校

(3) 通过网络进行德育

(4) 建立德育基地

九、班主任工作

【要求】

1. 识记班主任工作的基本任务和主要方法。

2. 理解班主任工作的意义、主要内容和对班主任素质的基本要求。

(一) 班主任工作的意义和班主任素质的基本要求

1. 班主任工作的意义

(1) 班主任是班集体的组织者和领导者

(2) 班主任是学生全面发展的促进者

(3) 班主任是联系班级中各任课老师的纽带

(4) 班主任是沟通学校与家庭、社会的桥梁

(5) 班主任是学校领导实施教育教学工作计划的得力助手和骨干

2. 班主任素质的基本要求

(1) 具有民主精神和友善态度

① 尊重信任学生，平易近人。

② 与人为善，宽容大度。

(2) 具有较广博的知识和较广泛的兴趣爱好

(3) 具有善于与学生沟通的能力

① 善于与学生相处。

② 具有开展班级工作的基本能力。

③ 具有健康的心理品质，包括积极的情绪、幽默感、自控能力等。

(二) 班主任工作的任务和内容

1. 班主任工作的基本任务

带好班级，教好学生。

2. 班主任工作的主要内容

(1) 对学生进行品德教育

(2) 教育学生努力学习，完成学习任务

(3) 指导学生课余生活，关心学生身体健康

(4) 组织学生参加劳动和其他社会活动

(5) 指导本班班委会和共青团、少先队工作

(6) 做好家访工作，争取社会有关方面的配合

(7) 评定学生操行

(三) 班主任工作的方法

1. 全面了解和研究学生

(1) 全面了解和研究学生是有效地进行班主任工作的前提和基础

(2) 了解和研究学生常用的方法有：考核法、观察法、测量法、问卷法、谈话法、实验法、调查法、访问法和书面材料分析法等

2. 组织和培养班集体

班集体是班主任工作的目的和结果，也是班主任开展工作的有力助手和途径，组织和培养班集体是班主任的中心工作。

培养班集体的主要途径有：

(1) 确立班集体的奋斗目标

(2) 选择和培养班干部

(3) 形成正确的集体舆论和培养良好的班风

(4) 组织多样的教育活动

3. 做好个别教育工作

(1) 个别教育同集体教育的关系

(2) 根据不同类型学生的实际，有针对性地做好个别学生，尤其是后进生的工作

4. 家庭教育与社会教育密切配合，统一各方面的教育力量

5. 做好班主任工作的计划和总结

(1) 班主任工作的计划

一般分为学期（或阶段）计划和具体活动计划。

(2) 班主任工作的总结

一般分为全面总结和专题总结。

十、课外校外教育

【要求】

1. 识记课外校外教育的概念、内容。

2. 理解课外校外教育的意义、主要特点。

3. 了解三结合教育的内容。

(一) 课外校外教育的概念和意义

1. 课外校外教育的概念

课外校外教育是指在课程计划和学科课程标准以外,利用课余时间,对学生实施的各种有目的、有计划、有组织的教育活动。

2. 课外校外教育的意义

(1) 课外校外教育有利于学生开阔眼界,获取新知识

(2) 课外校外教育是对青少年实施因材施教,发展个性特长的广阔天地

(3) 课外校外教育有利于发展学生智力,培养各种能力

(4) 课外校外教育是进行德育的重要途径

(二) 课外校外教育的内容和形式

1. 课外校外教育的主要内容

(1) 社会实践活动

(2) 学科活动

(3) 科技活动

(4) 文学艺术活动

(5) 文娱体育活动

(6) 社会公益劳动

(7) 课外阅读活动

2. 课外校外教育的组织形式

(1) 群众性活动

(2) 小组活动

（3）个人活动

（三）课外校外教育的特点和要求

1. 课外校外教育的主要特点

（1）自愿性

（2）灵活性

（3）实践性

2. 课外校外教育的主要要求

（1）要有明确的目的

（2）活动内容要丰富多彩，形式要多样化，要富于吸引力

（3）发挥学生的积极性、主动性，并与教师的指导相结合

（四）学校、家庭、社会三结合教育

1. 家庭教育

（1）家庭教育的特点

① 教育内容的生活化；② 教育方式的情感化；③ 教育方法的多样化。

（2）家庭教育的基本要求

① 创造和谐的家庭环境；② 对孩子的要求要合理、统一；③ 要理解和尊重孩子；④ 不断提高家长的文化素养和思想素养。

2. 社会教育

社会教育的途径和形式：① 社区对儿童和青少年的影响；② 各种校外机构的影响；③ 报刊、广播、电影、电视、戏剧等大众传播媒介的影响。

3. 学校、家庭、社会三结合，形成教育合力

（1）学校教育占主导地位

（2）家庭、社会和学校相互支持、目标一致

（3）加强学校与家庭之间的相互联系

其方式主要有：① 互相访问；② 建立通信联系；③ 举行家长会；④ 组织家长委员会；⑤ 举办家长学校。

（4）加强学校与社会教育机构之间的相互联系

其方式主要有：① 建立学校、家庭、社会三结合的校外教育组织；

② 学校与校外教育机构建立经常性的联系；③ 采取走出去、请进来的方法与社会各界保持密切联系。

心理学部分

一、绪论

【要求】

1. 了解心理学的发展历史、主要研究领域以及研究方法。

2. 理解心理活动的神经生理机制。

3. 掌握心理学的研究对象和研究目标。

（一）心理学的研究对象和研究目标

1. 心理学的研究对象

心理学是研究心理现象及其规律的科学。

2. 心理学的研究目标

陈述心理现象，解释心理现象，预测心理活动，调节与控制人的心理活动和行为。

（二）心理学的发展历史

1. 心理学发展的历史背景

2. 科学心理学的诞生

1879 年，德国哲学家和心理学家冯特在莱比锡大学建立了世界上第一个心理学实验室，从此心理学从哲学中分化出来成为一门独立的科学。

3. 心理学的主要流派

（1）结构主义心理学

（2）机能主义心理学

（3）行为主义心理学

（4）格式塔心理学

（5）精神分析学派

（6）人本主义心理学

（7）认知心理学

（三）心理学的研究领域和研究方法

1. 心理学的主要研究领域

（1）理论心理学

普通心理学、实验心理学、心理测量学、发展心理学、认知心理学、认知神经科学、人格心理学、社会心理学、变态心理学。

（2）应用心理学

教育心理学、咨询心理学、消费心理学、犯罪心理学、管理心理学、健康心理学。

2. 心理学研究的主要方法

（1）观察法

（2）实验法

（3）测验法

（4）调查法

（四）心理活动的神经生理机制

1. 神经系统的组成成分

（1）神经元与突触

（2）神经系统

① 周围神经系统；② 中枢神经系统；③ 大脑皮层主要功能定位。

2. 神经系统的活动方式与规律

（1）反射和反射弧；无条件反射和条件反射；第一信号系统和第二信号系统

（2）中枢神经活动的基本过程

（3）中枢神经活动的基本规律

二、感觉和知觉

【要求】

1. 识记感觉的概念和种类、知觉的概念和种类。

2. 理解感觉现象、知觉的基本特征、观察的品质。

3. 能够根据感觉和知觉的规律，分析具体的心理现象；能够运用感知规律，掌握促进直观教学的方法。

(一) 感觉

1. 感觉的概念

感觉是人脑对直接作用于感觉器官的客观事物的个别属性的反映。

2. 感觉的种类

(1) 外部感觉

① 视觉;② 听觉;③ 嗅觉;④ 味觉;⑤ 肤觉。

(2) 内部感觉

① 运动觉;② 平衡觉;③ 机体觉。

3. 感觉现象

(1) 适应

(2) 对比

(3) 后像

(4) 联觉

(二) 知觉

1. 知觉的概念

知觉是人脑对直接作用于感觉器官的客观事物的整体属性的反映。

2. 知觉的种类

(1) 根据知觉时起主导作用的感官的特性,分为视知觉、听知觉、嗅知觉、味知觉和触摸知觉。

(2) 根据知觉反映的客观对象的不同,分为空间知觉、时间知觉和运动知觉。

3. 知觉的基本特征

(1) 知觉的选择性

(2) 知觉的理解性

(3) 知觉的整体性

(4) 知觉的恒常性

(三) 观察

1. 观察的概念

观察是人有目的、有计划的知觉，是知觉的高级形式。

2. 观察的品质

(1) 观察的目的性

(2) 观察的客观性

(3) 观察的精细性

(4) 观察的敏锐性

3. 观察力的培养

① 明确观察的目的与任务；② 制订周密的观察计划；③ 具备观察事物的必要知识；④ 掌握一定观察方法；⑤ 学会观察记录；⑥ 观察后及时归纳与总结。

(四) 感知规律与直观教学

1. 直观教学的基本形式

(1) 实物直观

(2) 模象直观

(3) 言语直观

2. 遵循感知规律，促进直观教学

(1) 根据学习任务的性质，灵活运用各种直观方式

(2) 运用知觉的组织原则，突出直观对象的特点

(3) 指导学生掌握观察方法，养成良好的观察习惯

三、注意

【要求】

1. 识记注意的概念，注意的种类。

2. 理解注意的特征和功能。

3. 掌握注意的品质，能够运用注意规律组织教学活动。

(一) 注意概述

1. 注意的概念

注意是人的心理活动对一定对象的指向和集中。注意总是和各种心理活动紧密联系在一起，因此，注意是心理过程的积极状态，是心理活动的共同特性。

2. 注意的特征

(1) 指向性

(2) 集中性

3. 注意的功能

(1) 选择功能

(2) 保持功能

(3) 调节与监督功能

(二) 注意的种类

根据注意有无目的性和意志努力的程度，把注意分为不随意注意、随意注意和随意后注意。

1. 不随意注意(又称无意注意)

(1) 不随意注意的概念

不随意注意是事先没有预定目的，也不需要意志努力的注意。

(2) 引起不随意注意的原因

① 刺激物本身的特点；② 人本身的状态。

2. 随意注意(又称有意注意)

(1) 随意注意的概念

随意注意是一种自觉的、有预定目的的、必要时需要一定意志努力的注意。

(2) 引起随意注意的原因

① 对活动目的与任务的理解；② 对兴趣的依从性；③ 对活动的合理组织；④ 个性特点。

3. 随意后注意(又称有意后注意)

(1) 随意后注意的概念

随意后注意是指有预定目的，但不需要意志努力的注意。

(2) 随意后注意的特征

① 随意后注意服从于当前的活动目的与任务，但不需要意志努力；② 随意后注意是在随意注意基础上发展起来的；③ 随意后注意是注意的高级形式。

(三) 注意的品质

1. 注意广度

(1) 注意广度的概念

注意广度是在同一时间内意识能清楚地把握对象数量多少的注意品质。

(2) 影响注意广度的因素

① 知觉对象的特点;② 活动任务与知识经验。

2. 注意稳定性

(1) 注意稳定性的概念

注意稳定性是指注意能较长时间地保持在某种事物或某种活动上的注意品质。

(2) 影响注意稳定性的因素

① 对象本身的特点;② 活动的目的、任务;③ 人的主观状态。

3. 注意分配

(1) 注意分配的概念

注意分配是指人把自己的心理活动指向于两种或两种以上的对象或任务的注意品质。

(2) 影响注意分配的因素

① 从事活动的熟练程度;② 同时进行的几种活动的性质。

4. 注意转移

(1) 注意转移的概念

注意转移是指根据新任务的要求,主动地把注意从一个对象转移到另一个对象上去的注意品质。

(2) 影响注意转移的因素

① 原有活动吸引注意的程度;② 新的事物的性质与意义;③ 事先是否具有转移注意的信号;④ 个体的自控能力。

(四) 注意规律在教学中的运用

1. 不随意注意规律在教学中的运用

2. 随意注意规律在教学中的运用

3. 正确运用不随意注意和随意注意相互转换规律组织教学

四、记忆

【要求】

1. 识记记忆的概念、主要类型和基本过程，遗忘的概念。

2. 理解记忆系统的编码方式与存储特点，遗忘的基本规律，影响遗忘的因素，复习的作用。

3. 能够运用记忆规律，促进知识的巩固。

（一）记忆概述

1. 记忆的概念

记忆是人脑对过去经验的反映。用信息加工的术语来讲，记忆就是人脑对外界输入的信息进行编码、存储和提取的过程。

2. 记忆的基本过程

① 识记；② 保持；③ 回忆或再认。

3. 记忆的分类

（1）根据记忆的内容与经验的对象分类

① 形象记忆；② 情景记忆；③ 语义记忆；④ 情绪记忆；⑤ 运动记忆。

（2）根据信息保持时间的长短分类

① 瞬时记忆；② 短时记忆；③ 长时记忆。

（3）根据信息加工与存储的内容不同分类

① 陈述性记忆；② 程序性记忆。

（4）根据记忆时意识参与的程度分类

① 内隐记忆；② 外显记忆。

（二）记忆系统

1. 瞬时记忆（又称感觉记忆）

（1）瞬时记忆的概念

瞬时记忆是感觉性刺激作用后，在脑中继续短暂保持其映象的记忆。它以感觉痕迹的形式保存下来，所以又称感觉记忆。

（2）瞬时记忆的特点

（3）瞬时记忆的编码

① 编码方式;② 影响因素。

(4) 瞬时记忆的存储

① 存储容量;② 存储时间。

2. 短时记忆

(1) 短时记忆的概念

短时记忆是人脑中的信息保持在一分钟之内的记忆。

(2) 短时记忆的特点

(3) 短时记忆的编码

① 编码方式;② 影响因素。

(4) 短时记忆的存储

① 存储容量;② 存储时间。

3. 长时记忆

(1) 长时记忆的概念

长时记忆是指人脑对信息的保持时间在一分钟以上乃至终生的记忆。

(2) 长时记忆的特点

(3) 长时记忆的编码

① 编码方式;② 影响因素。

(4) 长时记忆的存储

① 存储容量;② 存储时间。

(三) 遗忘

1. 遗忘概述

(1) 遗忘的概念

遗忘是人脑对识记过的内容不能再认与回忆,或是错误再认与回忆。信息加工的观点认为,遗忘是信息提取不出或提取错误。

(2) 遗忘的种类

永久性遗忘和暂时性遗忘。

2. 遗忘的规律及影响遗忘进程的因素

(1) 艾宾浩斯遗忘曲线

(2) 影响遗忘进程的因素

①识记材料的性质；②识记材料的数量；③识记材料的序列位置；④学习程度。

3. 遗忘的原因

(1) 衰退说

(2) 干扰说(前摄抑制和倒摄抑制)

(3) 压抑(动机)说

(4) 提取失败说

4. 有效组织复习、减少遗忘的方法

(1) 及时复习

(2) 合理分配复习时间

(3) 分散复习与集中复习相结合

(4) 复习方式多样化

(5) 运用多种感官参与复习

(6) 尝试回忆与反复识记相结合

(四) 运用记忆规律，促进知识的巩固

1. 明确记忆的目的，增强学习主动性

2. 理解学习材料的意义，建立知识之间的内在联系

3. 对学习材料进行精加工，促进对知识的理解

4. 运用组块化学习策略，合理组织学习材料

5. 运用多种信息编码方式，提高信息加工处理的质量

6. 注重复习方法，防止知识遗忘

五、思维和想象

【要求】

1. 识记思维的概念、特征、基本过程和主要形式，想象的概念、种类。

2. 理解概念的形成、问题解决的阶段与影响因素、良好思维品质及其培养、想象的功能。

3. 能够联系实际，促进概念掌握，促进问题解决，培养创造性思维。

4. 运用想象规律指导教学。

(一) 思维概述

1. 思维的概念

思维是人脑对客观事物本质属性与内在联系的概括的、间接的反映。

2. 思维的特征

(1) 概括性

(2) 间接性

3. 思维与感知觉的关系

4. 思维的类型

(1) 根据思维的发展水平分类

① 动作思维;② 形象思维;③ 抽象逻辑思维。

(2) 根据思维的指向性分类

① 聚合思维;② 发散思维。

(3) 根据思维的逻辑性分类

① 直觉思维;② 分析思维。

(4) 根据思维的创造程度分类

① 常规性思维;② 创造性思维。

(二) 思维的过程和基本形式

1. 思维的过程

(1) 分析与综合

(2) 比较与归类

(3) 抽象与概括

(4) 系统化与具体化

2. 思维的基本形式

(1) 概念

(2) 判断

(3) 推理

3. 概念形成阶段

(1) 抽象化

(2) 类化

(3) 辨别

4. 科学概念的掌握

(1) 以感性材料作为概念掌握的基础

(2) 合理利用过去的知识与经验

(3) 充分利用“变式”

(4) 正确运用语言表达

(5) 形成正确的概念体系，并运用于实践中

(三) 问题解决

1. 问题与问题解决的特点

(1) 问题及其特点

(2) 问题解决及其特点

2. 解决问题的阶段

(1) 提出问题

(2) 分析问题

(3) 提出假设

(4) 检验假设

3. 影响问题解决的因素

(1) 人的知觉特点

(2) 定势与功能固着

(3) 原型启发

(4) 已有知识经验

(5) 情绪与动机

(6) 个性差异

(四) 创造性思维

1. 创造性思维概述

(1) 创造性思维的概念

创造性思维是产生具有社会价值的、新颖而独特的思维成果的过程，它与创造性活动紧密相联。

(2) 创造性思维的特征

① 思维与想象的有机统一；② 与创造性活动相联系；③ 常有“灵

感”出现；④ 发散思维和聚合思维相结合；⑤ 分析思维与直觉思维的统一。

2. 创造性思维的过程

(1) 准备期

(2) 酝酿期

(3) 豁朗期

(4) 验证期

3. 创造性思维的培养

(1) 运用启发式教学，激发学生的求知欲，调动学生的学习积极性

(2) 培养学生发散性思维和集中性思维

(3) 发展学生的创造性想象力

(4) 鼓励学生参加各项创造性活动，正确评价有创造力的学生

(五) 思维品质及其培养

1. 思维的品质

(1) 思维的广阔性和深刻性

(2) 思维的独立性和批判性

(3) 思维的逻辑性和严谨性

(4) 思维的灵活性和敏捷性

2. 良好思维品质的培养

(1) 加强科学思维方法论的训练

(2) 运用启发式进行教学，提高学生学习的积极性

(3) 加强言语交流训练

(4) 发挥定势的积极作用

(5) 培养解决实际问题的思考能力

(六) 想象

1. 想象的概念

想象是人脑对已有表象进行加工改造而形成新形象的心理过程。

2. 想象的功能

(1) 预见功能

(2) 补充功能

（3）代替功能

3. 想象的种类

（1）根据想象活动是否具有目的性分类

① 无意想象；② 有意想象。

（2）根据想象内容的新颖程度和形成方式对有意想象分类

① 再造想象；② 创造想象；③ 幻想。

4. 想象规律在教育教学中的运用

（1）在教学过程中发展学生的再造想象

① 再造想象是学生感知和掌握未知事物的有效手段；② 再造想象是学生理解和掌握客观事物规律与内在联系必不可少的心理条件；③ 再造想象是思想教育的重要形式之一。

（2）在教学活动过程中培养学生的创造性想象

① 丰富学生的表象储备；② 扩大学生的知识经验；③ 结合学科教学，有目的地训练学生的想象力；④ 引导学生进行积极的幻想。

六、情绪与意志

【要求】

1. 识记情绪的概念、分类和功能，意志的概念和基本特征。

2. 理解意志与认知过程、情绪过程的关系。

3. 掌握意志行动的心理过程、意志品质及其培养。

4. 联系实际，分析压力对身心健康的影响，调节和控制情绪的方法。

（一）情绪概述

1. 情绪的概念

情绪是人对客观事物是否符合自身需要而产生的态度体验。

2. 情绪的分类

（1）基本情绪的分类

① 快乐；② 悲哀；③ 愤怒；④ 恐惧。

（2）情绪状态的分类

① 心境；② 激情；③ 应激。

3. 情绪的功能

(1) 适应功能

(2) 动机功能

(3) 信息功能

(4) 组织功能

4. 情绪与认知过程

(二) 压力与应对方式

1. 压力

(1) 压力的概念

压力一般是指外界环境的变化和机体内部状态改变使人产生无法应对的负性情绪和信念。

(2) 压力与生理应激

① 警觉反应阶段;② 抗拒阶段;③ 衰竭阶段。

(3) 压力与心理反应

① 抑郁;② 焦虑;③ 恐惧;④ 狂躁。

2. 应对方式

(1) 应对方式的概念

(2) 应对方式的分类

(三) 情绪的调控与应用

1. 情绪的自我调节与控制

(1) 觉知自己的情绪状态

(2) 转移自己的注意

(3) 合理宣泄负面情绪

(4) 主动运用语言调节与控制自己的情绪

2. 健康情绪的培养

(1) 培养乐观向上的人生态度

(2) 培养广泛的兴趣和爱好

(3) 丰富积极的情绪体验

(4) 自我接纳和自我欣赏

(5) 建立良好的人际关系

（6）正确面对与处理负性情绪

（四）意志概述

1. 意志的概念

意志是自觉地确定目的，并根据目的来支配与调节行动，克服内、外部困难，实现预定目的的过程。

2. 意志的特征

3. 意志与认知过程、情绪过程的关系

（1）意志与认知过程的关系

（2）意志与情绪过程的关系

（五）意志行动的心理过程

1. 采取决定阶段

（1）动机斗争

① 双趋冲突；② 双避冲突；③ 趋避冲突；④ 双重趋避冲突。

（2）确定行动目标

2. 执行决定阶段

（1）行动方法和策略的选择

（2）克服困难实现所作出的决定

（六）意志品质及其培养

1. 意志品质

（1）自觉性

（2）果断性

（3）自制性

（4）坚韧性

2. 意志品质的培养

（1）加强目的性教育，确立崇高的理想

（2）组织实践活动，以取得意志锻炼的直接经验

（3）充分发挥班集体和榜样的教育作用

（4）启发学生加强意志的自我锻炼

（5）根据意志品质差异，采取不同的锻炼措施

七、需要与动机

【要求】

1. 识记需要的概念与类型,动机的概念与类型。

2. 理解马斯洛的需要层次理论和成败归因理论;了解其他动机理论。

3. 能够运用动机理论提出激发学生学习动机的具体措施。

(一) 需要与动机概述

1. 需要

(1) 需要的概念

需要是个体内部的某种缺乏或不平衡状态,是个体活动积极性的内在源泉。

(2) 需要的类型

① 生理需要和社会需要;② 物质需要和精神需要。

(3) 马斯洛的需要层次理论

① 生理需要;② 安全需要;③ 归属与爱的需要;④ 尊重的需要;⑤ 自我实现的需要。

2. 动机

(1) 动机的概念

动机是激发和维持有机体的行动,并使该行动朝向一定目标的心理倾向或内部驱力。

(2) 动机产生的条件

① 需要(内在条件); ② 诱因(外在条件)。

(3) 动机的类型

① 生理性动机和社会性动机;② 远景性动机和近景性动机;③ 主导动机和从属动机;④ 内部动机和外部动机。

(4) 动机的功能

① 引发功能;② 指向功能;③ 激励功能。

(5) 动机强度与工作效率:耶克斯-多德森定律

(二) 动机理论

1. 诱因理论

2. 期望价值理论

3. 成败归因理论

4. 成就目标理论

5. 成就动机理论

6. 自我效能感理论

（三）学习动机的激发

1. 创设问题情境，实施启发式教学

2. 根据作业难度，控制动机激奋水平

3. 利用反馈信息，有效进行奖惩

4. 合理设置课程，适当组织学习竞赛

5. 正确指导学习成绩的归因，促使学生继续努力学习

6. 提供成功的学习经验，增强学习的自我效能感

八、技能

【要求】

1. 识记技能的概念、特征和类型，动作技能、智力技能的概念和特点。

2. 理解动作技能和智力技能的形成阶段。

3. 掌握动作技能的形成条件和智力技能的培养要求。

（一）技能概述

1. 技能的概念

技能是个体运用已有的知识经验，通过练习而形成的合乎法则的活动方式。

2. 技能的特征

（1）技能是学习得来的，区别于本能行为

（2）技能是一种活动方式，区别于知识

（3）技能是合乎法则的活动方式，区别于一般的随意运动

3. 技能与习惯的区别

4. 技能的类型

（1）动作技能

① 动作技能的概念；② 动作技能的特点：动作对象的物质性，动作进行的外显性，动作结构的展开性。

（2）智力技能

① 智力技能的概念；② 智力技能的特点：动作对象的观念性，动作进行的内隐性，动作结构的简缩性。

（二）动作技能的形成

1. 动作技能的形成阶段

（1）动作的认知和定向阶段

（2）动作的模仿和联系阶段

（3）动作的整合、协调和完善阶段

2. 动作技能的形成条件

（1）动作概念掌握

（2）进行有效练习

（3）动作示范

（4）动作反馈

（三）智力技能的形成

1. 智力技能的形成阶段

（1）原型定向

① 原型定向的概念；② 教学要求。

（2）原型操作

① 原型操作的概念；② 教学要求。

（3）原型内化

① 原型内化的概念；② 教学要求。

2. 智力技能的培养要求

（1）确立合理的智力活动原型

（2）有效进行分阶段练习

① 激发学习的积极性和主动性；② 注意原型的完备性、独立性和概括性；③ 适应培养的阶段特征，正确使用言语；④ 注意学生的个性差异。

九、能力

【要求】

1. 识记能力的概念与分类，了解智力测验的标准及使用。

2. 理解智力结构，能力与知识、技能的关系，智力的主要理论，智商的测量。

3. 掌握能力的个别差异，影响智力发展的因素。

（一）能力概述

1. 能力的概念

能力是直接影响人的活动效率，使活动得以顺利进行的个性心理特征。

2. 能力与知识、技能的关系

（1）能力与知识、技能的区别

（2）能力与知识、技能的联系

3. 能力的分类

（1）一般能力和特殊能力

（2）认知能力、操作能力和社交能力

（3）模仿能力和创造能力

（二）智力的概念、理论及测验

1. 智力的概念

智力指的是一般能力。它是以抽象思维能力为核心的多种认知能力的综合。

2. 智力理论

（1）智力的因素理论

① 斯皮尔曼的二因素理论；② 瑟斯顿的群因素理论

（2）智力的结构理论（吉尔福特的三维结构理论）

（3）智力的形态理论（卡特尔的流体智力和晶体智力理论）

（4）智力的认知理论（斯腾伯格的智力三元结构理论）

（5）智力的多元理论（加德纳的多元智力理论）

3. 智力测验

(1) 常用的智力测验

① 比纳智力测验;② 韦克斯勒智力测验。

(2) 智力测验的标准

① 比率智商和离差智商的测定;② 智力测验的质量标准:信度,效度,标准化。

(3) 智力测验的使用

4. 影响智力发展的因素

(1) 遗传与营养

(2) 早期经验

(3) 教育与教学

(4) 社会实践

(5) 主观能动性

(三) 能力发展和能力的个别差异

1. 能力发展的一般趋势

2. 能力的个别差异

(1) 能力发展水平的差异

(2) 能力的类型差异

(3) 能力表现早晚的差异

十、人格

【要求】

1. 识记人格、气质和性格的概念。了解气质和人格理论、人格测验。

2. 理解人格的特点,气质和性格的特征及其相互关系,高级神经活动类型与气质类型的对应关系。

3. 根据实际,分析人格形成与发展的基本因素。

(一) 人格概述

1. 人格的概念

人格是构成一个人思想、情感及行为的特有模式,这个特有模式包含了一个人区别于他人的稳定而统一的心理品质。

2. 人格的特点

（1）人格的独特性

（2）人格的稳定性

（3）人格的整体性

（4）人格的功能性

（二）气质与性格

1. 气质

（1）气质的概念

气质是指一个人典型和稳定的心理活动的动力特征。

（2）气质的特性

① 感受性；② 耐受性；③ 反应的敏捷性；④ 可塑性；⑤ 情绪兴奋性；⑥ 内向与外向性。

（3）气质类型

① 胆汁质；② 多血质；③ 黏液质；④ 抑郁质。

（4）气质与高级神经活动类型的关系

2. 性格

（1）性格的概念

性格是指人对客观现实的稳定态度与习惯化了的行为方式相结合的人格特征。

（2）性格特征

① 态度特征；② 意志特征；③ 情绪特征；④ 理智特征。

（3）性格与气质的关系

① 性格与气质的联系；② 性格与气质的区别。

（三）人格理论

1. 人格的特质理论

（1）奥尔波特的人格特质理论

（2）卡特尔的人格特质理论

（3）艾森克的人格特质理论

（4）大五人格理论

2. 人格的精神分析理论

（1）弗洛伊德的人格理论

（2）荣格的人格理论

（3）阿德勒的人格理论

3. 人格的自我理论

（1）马斯洛的自我实现理论

（2）罗杰斯的健康人格理论

（四）人格测验

1. 自陈式人格测验

（1）明尼苏达多相人格测验

（2）爱德华个人兴趣量表

（3）卡特尔 16 种人格因素测验

（4）大五人格测验

2. 投射式人格测验

（1）罗夏墨迹人格测验

（2）主题统觉测验

（3）句子完成测验

（五）人格的形成与发展

1. 生物遗传因素

2. 家庭因素

3. 学校教育因素

4. 社会文化因素

5. 个人主观因素

十一、品德

【要求】

1. 识记品德的概念及其心理结构。

2. 理解品德形成的心理过程和品德形成理论。

3. 能够分析品德不良的原因；掌握矫正品德不良的方法。

（一）品德结构及其形成过程

1. 品德的概念

品德，又称道德品质，是个体依据一定的社会道德规范做出某种社会行为时所表现出来的比较稳定的心理特征和倾向。

品德的心理结构包括道德认识、道德情感、道德意志和道德行为。

2. 品德形成的心理过程

(1) 道德认识的形成

① 道德概念的掌握：感性道德表象的积累；道德知识的理解；道德概念的形成。② 道德评价能力的发展：从他律到自律；从对人到对己；从效果到动机；从片面到全面；从情景到原则。

(2) 道德情感的形成

(3) 道德意志的形成

(4) 道德行为的形成

(二) 品德形成理论

1. 道德发展阶段理论

(1) 皮亚杰的道德发展阶段论

(2) 科尔伯格的道德发展阶段论

2. 价值澄清理论

3. 社会学习理论

(三) 良好品德的培养

1. 晓之以理，提高认识

2. 动之以情，引起共鸣

3. 导之以行，落实行动

4. 持之以恒，坚持练习

(四) 学生品德不良的转化与矫正

1. 品德不良的表现：认识特征、情感特征、意志特征和行为特征

2. 品德不良的原因

(1) 客观原因

① 家庭不良影响和教育；② 学校工作的失误和学校生活中的不良影响；③ 社会环境的不良影响。

(2) 主观因素

① 缺乏正确的道德观念和信念；② 道德意志薄弱；③ 受不良行

为习惯的支配；④ 性格上的某些缺陷；⑤ 某些需要没有得到满足。

3. 品德不良的矫正方法

(1) 创设和谐的交流环境,了解学生不良行为的动机。

(2) 构建良好的心理气氛,消除疑惧心理与对立情绪。

(3) 善于发现“闪光点”,培养自信心。

(4) 把握转变关键时机,开展耐心细致工作。

(5) 提高分辨是非能力,形成正确是非观念。

(6) 锻炼学生与不良诱因作斗争的意志力,消除习惯惰性障碍。

(7) 根据学生的年龄特征和个别差异,采取灵活多样的教育措施。

十二、社会态度与行为

【要求】

1. 识记社会态度的概念、人际关系和群体心理的概念;了解态度理论。

2. 理解社会态度的功能、态度与行为的关系、社会印象形成效应、群体规范以及社会影响。

3. 能够根据有关态度的理论,结合实际生活,分析人的社会心理与社会行为。

(一) 社会态度

1. 社会态度概述

(1) 社会态度的概念

社会态度是个体基于过去经验对其周围的人、事、物持有的比较持久而一致的心理倾向。它包含认知成分、情感成分和行为意向成分。

(2) 社会态度的维度

2. 社会态度的功能

(1) 工具性功能

(2) 知识功能

(3) 价值表达功能

(4) 自我防御功能

(5) 社会适应功能

3. 态度与行为的关系

（二）态度理论

1. 态度的学习理论

2. 态度的分阶段形成理论

3. 态度的认知不协调理论

（三）印象形成及其效应

1. 印象形成概述

（1）印象形成的概念

印象形成是人在社会生活中形成并存储在记忆中的认知对象的形象。

（2）印象形成的模式

① 加法模式；② 平均模式；③ 加权平均模式。

2. 印象形成效应

（1）刻板印象

（2）首因效应和近因效应

（3）晕轮效应

（4）投射倾向

（四）人际关系

1. 人际关系概述

（1）人际关系的概念

人际关系是人们在社会生活过程中，在情感基础上形成的心理上的相互关系

（2）人际关系取向

① 包容需要；② 控制需要；③ 情感需要。

2. 人际吸引概述

（1）人际吸引的概念

人际吸引是个体之间在感情方面相互喜欢和亲和的现象。

（2）影响人际吸引的因素

① 外表；② 能力；③ 邻近；④ 相似；⑤ 互补；⑥ 性格特征。

（五）群体心理

1. 群体心理概述

(1) 群体心理的概念

(2) 群体规范

① 正式群体规范;② 非正式群体规范。

2. 社会促进和社会惰化

(1) 社会促进及其特征

(2) 社会惰化及其特征

3. 助人行为和侵犯行为

(1) 助人行为及其培养

(2) 侵犯行为及其控制

(六) 社会影响

1. 从众及其影响因素

(1) 从众的概念

从众是个体在群体的压力下,个人放弃自己的意见而采取与大多数人相一致的行为。

(2) 从众的原因

① 行为参照;② 偏离恐惧;③ 群体凝聚力。

(3) 从众的类型

① 行为上从众,内心也从众;② 行为上从众,内心不从众;③ 内心从众,行为不从众。

(4) 影响从众行为的因素

① 群体规模与特点;② 社会支持;③ 任务的熟悉程度;④ 性别。

2. 服从及其影响因素

(1) 服从的概念

服从是指个体按照社会要求、群体规范或他人的意志而作出的被迫行为。

(2) 影响服从的因素

① 他人的支持;② 对行为后果的意识;③ 个性因素。

3. 顺从及其影响因素

(1) 顺从的概念

顺从是指个体在行为上听从他人支配，接受别人指挥的心理现象。

（2）影响顺从的因素

① 个性因素；② 社会文化历史因素；③ 客观环境和群体压力因素。

十三、心理健康教育与心理咨询

【要求】

1. 识记心理健康和心理咨询的概念，了解心理健康的标准和心理咨询的目标。

2. 理解心理咨询与心理治疗、心理咨询与思想政治工作的关系，心理咨询的基本原则和基本步骤。

3. 运用心理咨询的有关方法和技术，分析和解决青少年常见的心理问题。

（一）心理健康

1. 心理健康的概念

心理健康是个体心理活动在自身及环境条件许可范围内所能达到的最佳功能状态。

2. 心理健康的标准

（1）心理健康的“自我实现者”标准

正视现实；接纳自我；言行坦率；热爱事业；独立独处；与环境关系和谐；欣赏日常生活；具有高峰体验；同情关心他人；人际关系深刻；待人民主平等；信守道德标准；富于幽默感；情绪积极稳定；人格结构完整。

（2）心理健康的现实标准

① 自我意识正确；② 人际关系协调；③ 性别角色分化；④ 情绪积极稳定；⑤ 社会适应良好；⑥ 人格结构完整。

3. 心理健康的促进

（1）促进心理健康的原则

① 生理与心理统一；② 个体与群体协调；③ 理论与实践结合；④ 防治与发展并重。

(2) 促进心理健康的途径与方法

① 开展心理健康教育;② 建立心理健康保健网络;③ 增设心理健康专业机构;④ 创造良好社会环境。

(二) 心理咨询

1. 心理咨询概述

(1) 心理咨询的概念

心理咨询是咨询师利用心理学原理与方法,通过与来访者建立相互信任的人际关系,给来访者以帮助、启发和教育,改变其认知、情感和态度,促进来访者人格发展和改善社会适应能力的过程。

(2) 心理咨询的特点

① 建立在咨询者与来访者良好的人际关系基础上;② 是一系列心理活动的过程。

2. 心理咨询与心理治疗的关系

(1) 心理咨询与心理治疗的联系

① 强调良好人际关系的建立;② 所遵循的理论、方法与原则一致。

(2) 心理咨询与心理治疗的区别

① 工作对象不同;② 遵循的模式不同;③ 工作任务的侧重面不同。

3. 心理咨询与思想政治工作的关系

(1) 心理咨询与思想政治工作的联系

① 思想上的一致性;② 组织上的联系性。

(2) 心理咨询与思想政治工作的区别

① 工作目标和范围不同;② 工作方法和手段不同;③ 遵循的理论和原则不同;④ 工作人员的专业方向不同;⑤ 工作效果的评估标准不同。

4. 心理咨询的目标

(1) 促使行为改变

(2) 改进应对技能

(3) 提高做决定的水平

(4) 改善人际关系

(5) 发展来访者的潜能

5. 心理咨询的原则、步骤和主要形式

(1) 心理咨询的基本原则

① 理解支持原则;② 保密原则;③ 倾听原则;④ 细致询问原则;⑤ 疏导原则;⑥ 促进成长原则;⑦ 预防原则。

(2) 心理咨询的基本步骤

① 建立关系;② 了解问题;③ 分析评估;④ 帮助指导;⑤ 结束咨询。

(3) 心理咨询的主要形式

① 直接咨询和间接咨询;② 个别咨询与小组咨询;③ 面谈咨询、信函咨询、电话咨询、现场咨询。

6. 心理咨询的主要理论与方法

(1) 精神分析理论

① 宣泄疗法;② 领悟疗法;③ 暗示疗法。

(2) 行为主义理论

① 系统脱敏;② 厌恶疗法;③ 强化、惩罚与消退法。

(3) 人本主义理论

① 当事人中心疗法;②"交朋友"小组——小团体心理治疗;③ 支持疗法。

(4) 认知行为理论

① 代表性观点——情绪的 A-B-C 理论;② 非理性信念的特征;③ 主要方法:非理性信念辨析;认知家庭作业;合理情绪想象。

(三) 青少年心理健康教育

1. 自我意识辅导

(1) 青少年自我意识的发展

(2) 青少年自我意识的教育

2. 人际交往辅导

(1) 青少年人际交往的特点

(2) 青少年人际交往的基本原则

3. 性别意识与异性交往辅导

(1) 青少年的性意识发展

(2) 青少年的异性交往教育

4. 考试焦虑辅导

(1) 考试焦虑的概念

(2) 考试焦虑的危害

① 降低学习效率；② 影响考试成绩；③ 形成焦虑型人格。

(3) 考试焦虑的矫正

① 自信训练；② 系统脱敏；③ 放松训练。

考试形式及试卷结构

试卷总分：150 分

考试时间：150 分钟

考试方式：闭卷，笔试

试卷内容比例：

教育学	50%
心理学	50%

试卷题型比例：

选择题	32%
辨析题	16%
简答题	32%
论述题	20%

样　　题

教　育　学

一、选择题:第 1～12 小题,每小题 2 分,共 24 分。在每小题给出的四个选项中,只有一项是最符合题目要求的。

1. 世界上最早的教育文献是

A.《学记》　　B.《论语》

C.《论演说家的教育》　　D.《理想国》

2. 教育目的在于通过"陶冶"和"唤醒"来培养儿童完整人格。主张这种观点的教育学派别是

A. 实验教育学　　B. 合作教育学

C. 批判教育学　　D. 文化教育学

3. 制约一个国家或地区教育领导权的主要因素是

A. 社会生产力　　B. 科学技术

C. 政治经济制度　　D. 主流文化

4. 有的家长让孩子在幼儿时就学习小学语文、数学等内容,导致一些孩子上小学后不想学习任何新知识,甚至变得性格孤僻。这些家长的做法违背了儿童身心发展规律中的

A. 个别差异性　　B. 阶段性

C. 不平衡性　　D. 稳定性

5. 关于教育要培养什么人的问题,2018 年全国教育大会明确提出

A. 培养德智体美全面发展的社会主义劳动者和接班人

B. 培养德智体美全面发展的社会主义建设者和接班人

C. 培养德智体美劳全面发展的社会主义劳动者和接班人

D. 培养德智体美劳全面发展的社会主义建设者和接班人

6. 我国近代第一个正式实施的学制是

A. 壬寅学制　　B. 癸卯学制

C. 壬子癸丑学制　　D. 壬戌学制

7.“教学有法,但无定法,贵在得法”。这种观点所体现的教师劳动的特点是

A. 主体性与示范性　　B. 连续性与广延性

C. 长期性与间接性　　D. 复杂性与创造性

8. 某初中教师在上课时发现男生小明正在给女同学递纸条,没收后发现纸条上写的是一封情书。为杜绝此类现象再次发生,他当堂公布了纸条内容。该教师的做法侵犯了小明的

A. 健康权　　B. 受教育权

C. 隐私权　　D. 公正评价权

9. 实现教育目的的主要途径是

A. 德育　　B. 班级管理

C. 教学　　D. 家校合作

10. 我国学校教学的基本组织形式是

A. 班级授课　　B. 分组教学

C. 个别教学　　D. 现场教学

11. 学校通过组织学生参观抗战遗址、观看抗日影视剧,培养其爱国主义情怀。这种德育方法属于

A. 说理教育法　　B. 实际锻炼法

C. 情感陶冶法　　D. 榜样示范法

12. 在教育合力形成过程中,占主导地位的因素是

A. 家庭教育　　B. 学校教育

C. 社会教育　　D. 社区教育

二、辨析题:第 13～14 小题,每小题 6 分,共 12 分。判断正误并给予简要说明。

13. 学生既是教育的对象也是教育的主体。

14. 提高全班学生成绩是班主任的中心工作。

三、简答题:第 15～17 小题,每小题 8 分,共 24 分。

15. 教育的相对独立性表现在哪些方面?

16. 简述一堂好课的基本标准。

17. 简述正面教育与纪律约束相结合原则的基本含义和贯彻要求。

四、论述题：第 18 小题，本题 15 分。

18. 阅读下列案例，并回答问题。

【案例】

网络环境下，多维的信息传递、交互的尝试学习与快捷的教学反馈，使不同层次的学生都能以适合自己的方式学习感兴趣的内容。如某小学在对“沙尘暴”的探究活动中，教师先将学生们反馈的共性问题“沙尘暴的发生”发送给学生进行集体讨论，又把学生们在网络上查到的大量图片发送给各学习小组进行合作学习，之后及时切换到个别化教学，就特定的问题，如沙尘暴的分布、变化及预测，扬沙、沙尘暴与浮尘的区别，沙尘暴与经济发展等，让学生进行个体交互式的探究学习，完成人—机、人—书、师—生、生—生的交互与沟通。

这样的教学不仅改变了学生的学习方式，提高了学习效率，而且更新了教师的教学观念，促进了教师的终身学习。一位教师说：“我简直是和学生赛跑，开始我对沙尘暴知之甚少，通过搜索引擎，找到很多资料，做到导航页上，在与学生一起研究的过程中，我又学到许多原来所不知的东西，网络的开放和便捷使我和学生处在同一起跑线上，不敢有一丝懈怠。”

（资料来源：梁杰，景洪春. 超越课堂的“课堂”[N]. 中国教育报，2003 - 12 - 30）

【问题】阐述现代化教学手段在教学中的作用，并结合案例进行分析。

心　理　学

五、选择题：第 19～30 小题，每小题 2 分，共 24 分。在每小题给出的四个选项中，只有一项是最符合题目要求的。

19. 标志心理学成为一门独立学科的事件是

A. 冯特建立心理学实验室　　　B. 华生提出 S—R 范式

C. 詹姆士出版《心理学原理》　　D. 巴甫洛夫创立条件反射学说

20. 下列选项中属于第二信号系统活动的是

A. 闻鸡起舞　　B. 谈虎色变

C. 见花落泪　　D. 触景生情

21. 知觉产生的基础是

A. 察觉　　B. 直觉

C. 感觉　　D. 联觉

22. 小雨通过观察和思考,总结出飞机、轮船、汽车、火车等都能运输物资或乘客。他的这种心理活动属于

A. 抽象　　B. 知觉

C. 联想　　D. 想象

23. 注意具有两个特性,它们是

A. 准备性和敏捷性　　B. 间接性和概括性

C. 形象性和新颖性　　D. 指向性和集中性

24. 情绪和情感所反映的是

A. 客观事物与动机的关系　　B. 客观事物与兴趣的关系

C. 客观事物与爱好的关系　　D. 客观事物与需要的关系

25. “中国肝胆外科之父”吴孟超曾多次表示:“我最大的幸福,也许是倒在手术台上。”他对工作的高度责任感和忘我精神属于性格的

A. 理智特征　　B. 意志特征

C. 情绪特征　　D. 态度特征

26. 下列选项中属于特殊能力的是

A. 记忆能力　　B. 绘画能力

C. 思维能力　　D. 想象能力

27. 小明仰望天空,以蓝天为背景看到白云像一座座雪山,而以白云做背景看到天空像蓝色海洋。这种对象和背景的转换体现了知觉的

A. 选择性　　B. 整体性

C. 理解性　　D. 恒常性

28. 一个外表充满魅力的人,其品行往往也会得到较高的评价。这种现象所反映的社会知觉效应是

A. 刻板效应　　B. 首因效应

C. 晕轮效应　　D. 投射效应

29. 由于外界环境变化或者机体内部状态改变而使人产生的无法应对的负性情绪或信念,称为

A. 文饰　　　　B. 退行

C. 否认　　　　D. 压力

30. 王强在工作和生活中总是公而忘私,尊老爱幼,乐于助人。这些特征体现的是

A. 品德　　　　B. 气质

C. 本能　　　　D. 理想

六、辨析题:第 31～32 小题,每小题 6 分,共 12 分。判断正误并给予简要说明。

31. 学生道德评价能力发展的规律之一是从他律到自律。

32. 技能就是习惯。

七、简答题:第 33～35 小题,每小题 8 分,共 24 分。

33. 简述短时记忆的特点。

34. 简述卡特尔的流体智力和晶体智力理论的主要内容。

35. 简述大五人格理论中的五种特质。

八、论述题:第 36 小题,本题 15 分。

36. 试述成败归因理论的基本内容以及其在激发学生学习动机中的运用。

参考答案

教育学

一、选择题

1. A　2. D　3. C　4. B　5. D　6. B　7.D

8. C　9. C　10. A　11. C　12. B

二、辨析题

13. **答案要点:**

正确。

学生是接受教育的人，是教育的对象；但学生不是被动接受教育的对象，是具有主观能动性的人，是学习的主人，也是教育的主体。

14. **答案要点：**

错误。

班主任是班级的教育者和组织者，组织和培养班集体是班主任的中心工作；提高学生成绩只是其工作任务之一。

三、简答题

15. **答案要点：**

（1）教育具有自身的继承关系；

（2）教育要受其他社会意识形态的影响；

（3）教育与社会政治经济发展不平衡；

（4）教育的独立性是相对的，不能将其绝对化。

16. **答案要点：**

（1）教师教的标准：教学目的明确；内容正确；结构合理；方法恰当；语言艺术；板书有序；教态从容自如。

（2）学生学的标准：学生注意力集中；思维活跃；积极参与；充分发挥自身特长。

17. **答案要点：**

（1）基本含义：

这一原则是指德育必须坚持正面教育，以说服教育为主，积极疏导，启发自觉，同时辅之以必要的纪律约束，引导学生的思想品德向正确方向健康发展。

（2）贯彻要求：

第一，坚持正面说理，运用正面榜样和事例教育学生，通过摆事实，讲道理，以理服人，启发自觉；

第二，以表扬、鼓励为主，批评、处分为辅，培养自尊心、上进心；

第三，建立必要的规章制度，并教育学生自觉遵守，逐步使他们建立良好的行为习惯，巩固为社会认可和赏识的行为习惯。

四、论述题

18. **答案要点：**

（1）教材建设的突破；

（2）教学组织形式的突破；

（3）师生关系的突破；

（4）提高了教学质量和教学效率；

（5）扩大了教学规模。

心　理　学

五、选择题

19. A　20. B　21. C　22. A　23. D　24. D

25. D　26. B　27. A　28. C　29. D　30. A

六、辨析题

31. **答案要点：**

正确。

低年级学生往往以成人的评价为依据来进行道德评价，随着年龄增长和知识经验的增加，慢慢学会依据自己的道德标准评价自己和他人。

32. **答案要点：**

错误。

技能是有意学习得来的，习惯是自然习得的；技能形成与情景和任务相关，习惯只和情景联系；技能有水平高低之分，无好坏之别，而习惯无高低之分，有好坏之别。

七、简答题

33. **答案要点：**

（1）信息保持时间短，最长不超过1分钟。

（2）记忆容量有限，一般为7±2个组块。

（3）短时记忆的信息容易受干扰。

34. **答案要点：**

（1）流体智力主要是指对新奇事物的快速辨识、记忆、理解能力；晶体智力主要指运用已有知识和技能去吸收新知识或解决问题的能力。

（2）流体智力主要受人的生物因素的影响，发展到一定年龄会停滞、衰退；晶体智力则与教育和知识经验有关，一般来说随年龄增长而增长。

35. **答案要点：**

（1）开放性。

（2）宜人性。

（3）责任心。

（4）神经质。

（5）外倾性。

八、论述题

36. **答案要点：**

（1）心理学家韦纳将活动成败的原因归结为以下几个主要因素：能力高低、努力程度、任务难易、运气好坏等；这些因素又可以归为三个维度：内外维度、稳定性维度和可控性维度。

韦纳认为，每一维度对动机都有重要的影响。在内外维度上，如果将成功归因于内部因素，会产生自豪感，从而动机提高；归因于外部因素，则会产生侥幸心理。将失败归因于内部因素，则会产生羞愧感；归因于外部因素，则会生气。在稳定性维度上，如果将成功归因于稳定因素，会产生自豪感，从而动机提高；归因于不稳定因素，则会产生侥幸心理。将失败归因于稳定因素，则会产生绝望感；归因于不稳定因素，则会生气。在可控性维度上，如果将成功归因于可控因素，则会积极地去争取成功；归因于不可控因素，则不会产生多大的动力。将失败归因于可控因素，则会继续努力；归因于不可控因素，则会绝望。

（2）根据该理论，良好的归因模式可影响学生的学习动机。因此，在激发学生学习动机时，一方面要引导学生进行正确归因和积极归因；另一方面可以对学习困难学生进行归因训练，引导学生将成败归因为努力程度。